# KAFFE FASSETT'S
# *Quilt Grandeur*

**20 designs from Rowan for patchwork and quilting**

*featuring*

Liza Prior Lucy • Pauline Smith
Roberta Horton • Mary Mashuta
Judy Baldwin • Corienne Kramer
Sally Davis • Brandon Mably

The Taunton Press

R O W A N

**The Taunton Press**
Inspiration for hands-on living®

The Taunton Press, Inc., 63 South Main Street,
PO Box 5506, Newtown, CT 06470-5506
email: tp@taunton.com

First published in Great Britain in 2013 by
Rowan
Green Lane Mill
Holmfirth
West Yorkshire
England HD9 2DX

Copyright © Westminster Fibers, Inc. 2013
3430 Toringdon Way, Suite 301
Charlotte, NC 28277
U.S.A

Patchwork designs      Kaffe Fassett, Liza Prior Lucy, Pauline Smith, Roberta Horton, Mary Mashuta, Judy Baldwin, Sally Davis, Corienne Kramer, Brandon Mably

| | |
|---|---|
| Art director/styling | Kaffe Fassett |
| Editor | Pauline Smith |
| Technical editor | Ruth Eglinton |
| Designer | Anne Wilson |
| Location photography | Debbie Patterson |
| Still photography | Dave Tolson |
| Illustrations | Ruth Eglinton |
| Quilters | Judy Irish, Pauline Smith |

Publishing consultant   Susan Berry

Library of Congress Cataloging-in-Publication Data in progress

ISBN 978-1-62113-976-8

Color reproduction and printing by KHL Chromagraphics and KHL Printing Co Pte Ltd, Singapore

10 9 8 7 6 5 4 3 2 1

# Contents

# A very English setting

Every year when we start planning our next Rowan patchwork book I try to find a colourful location that has many moods to suit our varying collection of quilts. I also want to make each book different from the previous ones in the series. Our last three books were photographed respectively in the exotic locations of Provence, France;  Skansen Museum in Sweden and Bulgaria. I felt this time a very English setting would feel fresh. Brandon and I scanned the location sites and settled on the historic and grand Cornish estate of Port Eliot. We loved the fact the rooms had rich-coloured wall treatments including a panoramic mural. There was also a light-filled orangery with handsome sage-coloured lattice work and white marble busts.

When we did our recce before the shoot, we found many more delightful features and, best of all, discovered that the owner, Lady St Germans, was an admirer of my design work and was keen to learn to stitch needlepoint! Since the house is open to the public for limited periods each year we were afraid it might be turn out to look like a stage set. To our relief, though, it was very much a lived-in family house on  a grand country scale. So the wear and tear of living with dogs, house guests and the visiting public softened the antique grandeur to something

much more human, which both the owners and I myself find so appealing. The deliciously relaxed approach to the ageing of furnishings, allowing the sometimes frayed and worn surfaces to have a natural patina afforded us so many contrasts of background for our quilts. Ranging from rich crimson damask rooms with tortoiseshell carbonates to pale aqua and beige papered walls hung with gold-framed family portraits to the vast garden landscaping, we were spoiled for choice. Best of all they left the three of us – photographer Debbie, Brandon and myself – to have the run of the house to do  do our shoot as we pleased. It proved one of the richest settings for our books to date and contrasts wonderfully with the humble farming village scenes of our last book.

Since we already had the location in mind, some of our quilts were made specifically to chime with it, so have an antique old-world colouring. My *Misty Log Cabin*, *Overlapping Squares* and especially Liza's *Dreamy Hexagons* capture the subtleties of the marble tables and the sage-green latticework of the orangery. The vibrant mural became a great setting for our brighter, bolder quilts and the blue-green swimming pool the perfect place for our watery-blue quilts while the golden-brown glow of leather-bound volumes in the drawing room set off our more honey-toned quilts.

PORT ELIOT.   ST. GERMANS.   CORNWALL.

F.A.O:-
Accounts Dept
Port Eliot Estate Office
Port Eliot, St Germans
Saltash
CORNWALL
PL 12

# the fabrics

This time we have chosen to showcase a selection of the current fabrics by Kaffe, Philip Jacobs and Brandon Mably in grouped palettes (rather than individually) alongside the classic fabrics that might go with them in a quilt. We hope this makes it easier for you to find a replacement fabric should you be unable to find the one you are looking for.

## Soft reds

◄ **Classic range**
GP89 Asian Circles tomato
GP70 Spot red
SC07 Shot Cotton persimmon
SC81 Shot Cotton magenta
GP91 Big Blooms red
GP70 Spot magenta
GP59 Guinea Flower tomato

**Current range** ►
PJ52 Picotte Poppies red
PJ56 Floating Mums magenta
PJ57 Painted Daisy magenta
GP129 Oriental Trees magenta
GP132 Camellia pink
PJ51 Brassica red

# Garden

◀ **Classic range**
GP51 Shirt Stripes green
GP70 Spot green
SC92 Shot Cotton cactus
GP89 Asian Circles green
GP70 Spot apple
SC43 Shot Cotton lime
GP71 Aboriginal Dot leaf
GP70 Spot pond

**Current range** ▶
GP91 Big Blooms emerald
PJ51 Brassica green
GP131 Jupiter green
PJ59 Banded Poppy sage
GP132 Camellia green
GP129 Oriental Trees green

## Autumn

◀ **Classic range**
GP59 Guinea Flower brown
GP89 Asian Circles orange
GP71 Aboriginal Dot terracotta
Caterpillar Stripe yellow
SC80 Shot Cotton clementine
GP117 Ombre brown
GP71 Aboriginal Dot pumpkin
Narrow Stripe red
SC54 Shot Cotton bordeaux

**Current range** ▶
GP131 Jupiter brown
GP130 Peking rust
GP128 Chard autumn
BM35 Lotto ochre
PJ55 Feathers brown
PJ52 Picotte Poppies ochre

# Blues

◀ **Classic range**
GP92 Millefiore blue
SC45 Shot Cotton true cobalt
SC41 Shot Cotton jade
Caterpillar Stripe blue
GP20 Paperweight cobalt
GP70 Spot sapphire
GP51 Shirt Stripe cobalt
GP117 Ombre blue

**Current range** ▶
PJ58 Lacy blue
GP130 Peking blue
BM36 Nets blue
GP132 Camellia blue
BM38 Flutter periwinkle
PJ51 Brassica blue
GP128 Chard blue

# substituting fabrics

## Pauline Smith

Now and again, you may need to find replacements for some of the fabrics, as some tend to go out of stock more quickly than others. It even happens to Kaffe!

He begins designing his quilts for each book roughly eighteen months before the book is in the shops. This early start is necessary to fit in with his busy schedule, as he's often away for weeks at a time, giving lectures and doing workshops. Occasionally some of his first choice fabrics cannot be guaranteed to be available when the book is launched but with such a wide range of Rowan fabrics, and with new designs and colourways added twice a year, suitable replacements can always be found.

On the opposite page are two examples of how Kaffe went about making such substitutions for his designs in this book.

**Doing your own substitutions**
- When substituting fabric, first look at the fabric in the context of the overall quilt design. Ask yourself the following questions:
- Does the substitute sit well with the other fabrics in the quilt?
- Is it a key fabric (ie a fussy-cut floral) or a more restrained background fabric (important perhaps in giving space to more flamboyant prints) or an accent fabric that adds a spark to the whole design.
- It may be you'll have to swop more than one fabric to make a harmonious new arrangement, so it pays to have a flexible approach and be prepared to make more changes than you first thought.

A flannel design wall (see Glossary on page 146) would be a huge help as it allows you to assess your design using cut pieces of fabric that can be placed in position simply by pressing them firmly to the flannel. They can be removed easily if they aren't right. A reducing glass (see Glossary on page 146) is another useful piece of equipment, as it allows you to see the whole composition at a glance, showing up any wrong fabric choices instantly. It's worth spending time making sure you're happy with arrangement at this stage, as there's nothing worse than having to unpick blocks because you didn't stand back and take a good look before starting to piece the quilt.

If you find a good fabric design as a substitute but the colours are a bit strong, flipping the fabric to use the wrong side gives a faded antique effect that can be very useful. Kaffe used this technique in his Overlapping Squares quilt when he flipped turquoise Asian Circles and grey Begonia Leaves. These two fabrics are used right side up in the quilt as well.

ABOVE Asian Circles right and wrong sides
BELOW Begonia Leaves right and wrong sides

## Mirror Squares

Kaffe substituted fabrics in this quilt (see page 20) when he realized that his original fabric choices of Bekah (in plum) and Plink (in rust) might not be available long term. At this stage the quilt had been pieced but not quilted, thankfully.

So how does he make these substitutions? To replace Bekah (in plum) his first thought was to try August Rose (in purple). Replacement squares were cut and pinned into place, but Kaffe found that because the lilac shade in the roses was too light it was distracting – the eye was drawn to the light lilac rather than taking in the the quilt as a whole. So he abandoned that idea and then tried Frilly (in orange) – not an obvious choice to replace a purple fabric! However, the saturated colour blended harmoniously with the other fabrics and the distraction problem was solved.

Grandiflora (in tomato) proved be the perfect replacement for Plink (in rust). In fact, Kaffe preferred it to the Plink.

**LEFT**
Top: Frilly
Middle: August Rose
Bottom: Bekah

**ABOVE**
Top: Grandiflora
Bottom: Plink

**RIGHT AND FAR RIGHT**
Top: Rings
Bottom: Plink

**BELOW**
Top: Millefiore
Bottom: Paisley Jungle

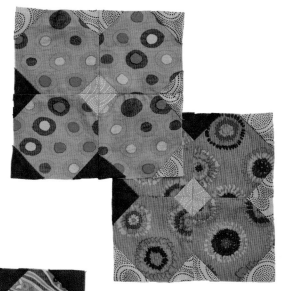

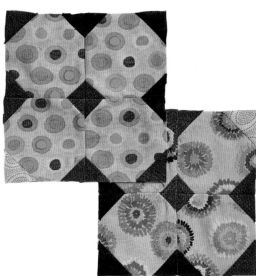

## Amber Snowball

This quilt had similar issues to Mirror Squares but in this case the fabrics that needed to be substituted were two colourways of Plink (in magenta and sand) and Paisley Jungle (in tangerine).

Plink is a small-scale circular design so Kaffe thought Brandon's Rings (in pink and taupe) would be perfect matches. Paisley Jungle (in tangerine) was swopped for Millefiore (in orange), once again a perfect match.

13

## *Dotty Frames*
by Kaffe Fassett

Loving dots of all sorts, I chose as many as I could that went together from the Kaffe Fassett Collective for my *Dotty Frames* quilt. The threadbare drapes in an upstairs bedroom made a great setting.

## *Amber Snowball*
by Kaffe Fassett

I couldn't believe my luck when I saw how well my Amber Snowball quilt fitted into the floral drama of the Mural Room. The books on the mantle are a *trompe l'oeil* – they are actually carved from wood.

## *Shadow Pinwheel*
### by Kaffe Fassett

The jolly tones of my *Shadow Pinwheel* breathe some exciting
modern life into the grand Mural Room.

***Mirror Squares***
by Kaffe Fassett

The design of this quilt
creates a great vehicle for
our large prints, and I think
my *Mirror Squares* goes
perfectly in this country
setting.

*Espania*
by Kaffe Fassett

This gorgeous antique bed made the perfect setting for my *Espania* quilt. The effect is exactly what I wanted – splendidly operatic!

23

## Overlapping Squares
### by Kaffe Fassett

As we had already visited Port Eliot during a pre-photography recce, I designed the palette of my Overlapping Squares quilt to echo the delicate colouring of the wallpapers at the house. It worked a treat!

## *Misty Log Cabin*
by Kaffe Fassett

Loving a soft grey palette, I designed this *Misty Log Cabin* to showcase our new grey prints. I think it works really well with the weathered stones and tree bark at Port Eliot.

## Rick Rack
by Kaffe Fassett

The fluted carvery on this ancient stone arch at the Chapel at Port Eliot makes the perfect foil for the bold zigzags of my Rick Rack quilt.

## *Double Diamond*
### by Kaffe Fassett

The elegant orangery with its subtle greens makes gives my *Double Diamond* quilt all the delight of a vista of spring flowers.

## *Geese in Flight*
by Roberta Horton

The electric blue walls of the kitchen bring Roberta Horton's *Geese in Flight* quilt to startling life. It looks equally good in the dining room too.

## *Lorna Doone*
by Corienne Kramer

The delicate watercolour palette of Corienne Kramer's quilt melts into this grand British setting. Appropriately the quilt sports the name *Lorna Doone*: she was a West Country heroine too.

### Dreamy Hexagons
by Liza Prior Lucy

This quilt of Liza Prior Lucy's is a triumph of subtle pale tones. It looks completely at home in this most English of settings.

## Diagonal Bricks
by Judy Baldwin

Judy Baldwin's *Diagonal Bricks* settles in harmoniously with these first editions and in the cobblestoned side entrance.

OVERLEAF

## *Cartwheel*
by Liza Prior Lucy

Liza Prior Lucy's *Cartwheel* quilt is bold and rich enough to hold its own against the wonderful colours of Port Eliot's historic mural.

## *Marmalade*
by Liza Prior Lucy

The glowing oranges, pinks and reds of Liza Prior Lucy's *Marmalade* quilt really glows out against the baroque architecture and the tortoiseshell of the sitting room.

## Paper Dolls
by Brandon Mably

Brandon Mably's wonderfully lively *Paper Dolls* child's quilt
does a merry dance against the more restrained setting of
the orangery.

## Traffic Jam
by Pauline Smith

Pauline Smith's delightful *Traffic Jam* quilt lights up in the drawing room. In the detail picture, you can see Lady Catherine taking a delighted Brandon for a ride in her jeep!

## Blue Haze
by Pauline Smith

Looking just like a cool
tile panel at Port Eliot's
pool, the *Blue Haze* quilt
by Pauline Smith blends
beautifully with this setting.

### *Swirling Petals*
by Mary Mashuta

Mary Mashuta's *Swirling Petals* quilt with its soft forms is echoed in the lush hydrangeas by the Chapel.

51

### Meadow Pathways
by Sally Davis

The tonal elegance of Sally Davis' *Meadow Pathways* quilt echoes the symmetry of the latticework in Port Eliot's orangery.

# dotty frames *

### Kaffe Fassett

The block centres in this quilt are large squares (Large Square) surrounded with a narrow frame made using 2 rectangles (Long and Short Rectangle), all are cut to size and no templates are provided for this very simple design. The blocks, which finish to 9½in (24.25cm) are set in straight rows interspaced and surrounded with sashing strips and corner posts (Sashing and Corner Post), which are again cut to size.

## SIZE OF QUILT
The finished quilt will measure approx. 78½in x 78½in (199.5cm x 199.5cm).

## MATERIALS
### Patchwork Fabrics
PAPERWEIGHT
| | | |
|---|---|---|
| Pastel | GP20PT | ¼yd (25cm) |

GUINEA FLOWER
| | | |
|---|---|---|
| Blue | GP59BL | ⅝yd (60cm) |
| White | GP59WH | ⅝yd (60cm) |

SPOT
| | | |
|---|---|---|
| China Blue | GP70CI | ⅝yd (60cm) |
| Lilac | GP70LI | ⅜yd (35cm) |
| Midnight | GP70MD | ¼yd (25cm) |
| Sky Blue | GP70SK | ⅜yd (35cm) |
| Tomato | GP70TM | ⅜yd (35cm) |

ASIAN CIRCLES
| | | |
|---|---|---|
| Green | GP89GN | ½yd (45cm) |

MILLEFIORE
| | | |
|---|---|---|
| Lilac | GP92LI | ¼yd (25cm) |
| Pastel | GP92PT | ¼yd (25cm) |

BRASSICA
| | | |
|---|---|---|
| Pastel | PJ51PT | ½yd (45cm) |

PICOTTE POPPIES
| | | |
|---|---|---|
| Natural | PJ52NL | ¼yd (25cm) |

CACTUS DAHLIAS
| | | |
|---|---|---|
| Pastel | PJ54PT | ¼yd (25cm) |

### Sashing Fabric
SPOT
| | | |
|---|---|---|
| White | GP70WH | 2yd (1.8m) |

### Backing Fabric  5¾yd (5.25m)
We suggest these fabrics for backing
PICOTTE POPPIES  Natural, PJ52NL
PAPERWEIGHT  Pastel, GP20PT
GUINEA FLOWER  White, GP59WH

### Binding
SPOT
| | | |
|---|---|---|
| White | GP70WH | ¾yd (70cm) |

### Batting
86in x 86in (218.5cm x 218.5cm)

### Quilting thread
Toning machine quilting thread and toning perlé embroidery thread

## Templates

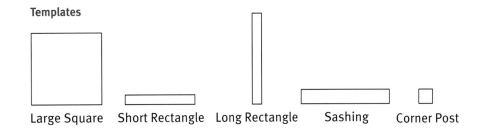

Large Square   Short Rectangle   Long Rectangle   Sashing   Corner Post

## CUTTING OUT
**Large Squares**  Cut 8in (20.25cm) strips across the width of the fabric. Each strip will give you 5 squares per full width. From the strips cut 8in (20.25cm) squares. Cut 8 in PJ51PT, 6 in GP89GN, 5 in GP20PT, GP59BL, GP59WH, GP92LI, GP92PT, PJ52NL and PJ54PT. Total 49 squares.

**Long Rectangles**  Cut 1½in (3.75cm) strips across the width of the fabric. Each strip will give you 4 rectangles per full width. Cut 1½in x 10in (3.75cm x 25.5cm) rectangles. Cut 24 in GP70CI, 14 in GP59BL, GP70SK, 12 in GP59WH, GP70LI, GP70TM and 10 in GP70MD. Total 98 rectangles.

**Short Rectangles**  Cut 1½in (3.75cm) strips across the width of the fabric. Each strip will give you 5 rectangles per full width. Cut 1½in x 8in (3.75cm x 20.25cm) rectangles. Cut 24 in GP70CI, 14 in GP59BL, GP70SK, 12 in GP59WH, GP70LI, GP70TM and 10 in GP70MD. Total 98 rectangles.

**Sashing**  Cut 2in (5cm) strips across the width of the fabric. Each strip will give you 4 sashing strips per full width. Cut 2in x 10in (5cm x 25.5cm) rectangular sashing strips. Cut 112 in GP70WH.

**Corner Posts**  Cut 2in (5cm) strips across the width of the fabric. Each strip will give you 20 corner posts per full width. From the strips cut 2in (5cm) squares. Cut 64 in GP70WH.

**Binding**  Cut 9 strips 2½in (6.5cm) across the width of the fabric in GP70WH.

**Backing**  Cut 2 pieces 40in x 86in (101.5cm x 218.5), 2 pieces 40in x 7in (101.5cm x 17.75cm) and 1 piece 7in x 7in (17.75cm x 17.75cm) in backing fabric.

## MAKING THE BLOCKS
Use a ¼in (6mm) seam allowance throughout. Referring to the quilt assembly diagram for fabric placement piece 49 blocks as shown in block assembly diagram a, the finished block can be seen in diagram b.

## BLOCK ASSEMBLY DIAGRAMS

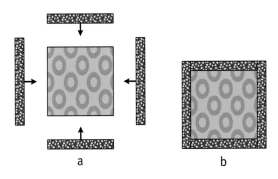

a                          b

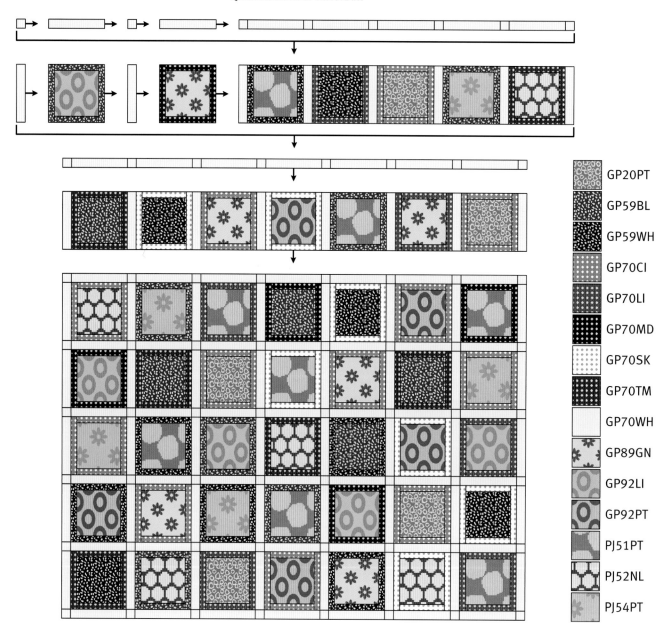

| | |
|---|---|
| | GP20PT |
| | GP59BL |
| | GP59WH |
| | GP70CI |
| | GP70LI |
| | GP70MD |
| | GP70SK |
| | GP70TM |
| | GP70WH |
| | GP89GN |
| | GP92LI |
| | GP92PT |
| | PJ51PT |
| | PJ52NL |
| | PJ54PT |

**MAKING THE QUILT**

Lay out the blocks and interspace with the sashing and corner posts as shown in the quilt assembly diagram. Separate into 15 rows and piece the rows. Join the rows to complete the quilt.

**FINISHING THE QUILT**

Press the quilt top. Seam the backing pieces using a ¼in (6mm) seam allowance to form a piece approx. 86in x 86in (218.5cm x 218.5cm). Layer the quilt top, batting and backing and baste together (see page 144). Using toning machine quilting thread stitch in the ditch in all the seams, then using toning perlé embroidery thread, quilt diagonal lines in each large square to from an 'X'. Trim the quilt edges and attach the binding (see page 145).

# shadow pinwheel *

### Kaffe Fassett

The first block in this quilt is a simple half-square triangle block made with a large triangle (Template F). The second block is a pinwheel made using a small triangle (Template G). The blocks are alternated throughout the quilt centre, set into straight rows. The centre is then surrounded with a border of half square triangle blocks with a pinwheel at each corner to complete the quilt.

## SIZE OF QUILT
The finished quilt will measure approx. 80in x 96in (203.25cm x 243.75cm).

## MATERIALS
**Patchwork Fabrics**
CABBAGE AND ROSE

| | | |
|---|---|---|
| Wine | GP38WN | ⅞yd (80cm) |

SPOT

| | | |
|---|---|---|
| Apple | GP70AL | ⅝yd (60cm) |
| Duck Egg | GP70DE | ⅝yd (60cm) |
| Ice | GP70IC | ¾yd (70cm) |
| Orange | GP70OR | ¾yd (70cm) |
| Peach | GP70PH | ½yd (45cm) |
| Royal | GP70RY | ¾yd (70cm) |

ABORIGINAL DOTS

| | | |
|---|---|---|
| Iris | GP71IR | ⅞yd (80cm) |
| Lilac | GP71LI | ¾yd (70cm) |
| Ochre | GP71OC | ⅞yd (80cm) |
| Silver | GP71SV | ½yd (45cm) |

PLINK

| | | |
|---|---|---|
| Red | GP109RD | ½yd (45cm) |

BRASSICA

| | | |
|---|---|---|
| Green | PJ51GN | ⅝yd (60cm) |

PICOTTE POPPIES

| | | |
|---|---|---|
| Red | PJ52RD | ¾yd (70cm) |

GRANDIFLORA

| | | |
|---|---|---|
| Purple | PJ53PU | ¾yd (70cm) |

FEATHERS

| | | |
|---|---|---|
| Red | PJ55RD | ⅞yd (80cm) |

**Backing Fabric** 7yd (6.4m)
We suggest these fabrics for backing
CABBAGE AND ROSE Fuchsia, GP38FU
PICOTTE POPPIES Red, PJ52RD

**Binding**
SAND DOLLARS

| | | |
|---|---|---|
| Red | BM31RD | ⅞yd (80cm) |

**Batting**
88in x 104in (223.5cm x 264.25cm)

**Quilting thread**
Toning machine quilting thread

## Templates

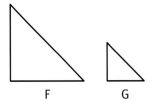

F            G

## CUTTING OUT
**Template F** Cut 8⅞in (22.5cm) strips across the width of the fabric, Each strip will give you 16 triangles per full width. Cut 8⅞in (22.5cm) squares, then cut each square diagonally to form 2 triangles using the template as a guide. Handle the triangles carefully as the long edge will be on the bias and stretchy. Cut 16 in GP38WN, 15 in GP71LI, 11 in GP70IC, GP70OR, GP71OC, PJ53PU, 10 in GP70RY, PJ52RD, 9 in GP71IR, PJ51GN, PJ55RD, 8 in GP70AL, GP71SV, 6 in GP70DE, 4 in GP70PH and GP109RD. Total 152 triangles.
**Template G** 4⅞in (12.5cm) strips across the width of the fabric, Each strip will give you 16 triangles per full width. Cut 4⅞in (12.5cm) squares, then cut each square diagonally to form 2 triangles using the template as a guide. Handle the triangles carefully as the long edge will be on the bias and stretchy. Cut 40 in GP71OC, 36 in GP71IR, PJ55RD, 28 in GP70DE, 24 in GP70AL, GP70RY, 20 in GP38WN, PJ53PU, 16 in GP70IC, GP70OR, GP70PH, GP71LI, GP71SV, GP109RD, PJ52RD and 12 in PJ51GN. Total 352 triangles.

**Binding** Cut 10 strips 2½in (6.5cm) wide across the width of the fabric in BM31RD.

**Backing** Cut 2 pieces 40in x 104in (101.5cm x 264.25cm), 2 pieces 40in x 9in (101.5cm x 22.75cm) and 1 piece 25in x 9in (63.5cm x 22.75cm) in backing fabric.

## MAKING THE BLOCKS
Use a ¼in (6mm) seam allowance throughout. Refer to the quilt assembly diagram for fabric placement. First join the template F triangles in pairs to form squares as shown in diagram a. Handle the triangles carefully and take care not to stretch the diagonal seam as you sew. Make a total of 76 blocks as shown in diagram b, 40 for the quilt centre and 36 for the border.

Next join the template G triangles to form squares as shown in diagram C. Make 4 identical squares for each pinwheel and join as shown in diagram d. The finished pinwheel is shown in diagram e. Make a total of 44 pinwheels, 40 for the quilt centre and 4 for the border corner posts. There is one block close to the centre of the quilt made using GP109RD (Plink Red) and GP70RY (Spot Royal) where the reverse of the Plink Red (GP109RD) fabric was used as Kaffe wanted a softer look in this position.

## MAKING THE QUILT
Lay out the blocks into 10 rows of 8 blocks, alternating the blocks as shown in the quilt

## BLOCK ASSEMBLY DIAGRAMS

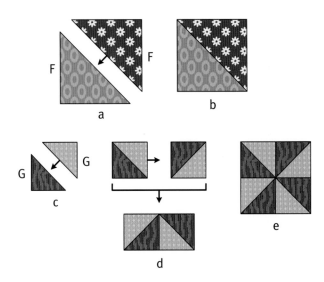

assembly diagram. Note that the diagonal seams of the half-square triangle blocks run top left to bottom right throughout the quilt centre, but in the opposite direction for the borders. Join the rows to complete the quilt centre. Piece the side borders and join to the quilt centre, then piece the top and bottom borders and join to the centre to complete the quilt.

**FINISHING THE QUILT**
Press the quilt top. Seam the backing pieces using a ¼in (6mm) seam allowance to form a piece approx. 88in x 104in (223.5cm x 264.25cm). Layer the quilt top, batting and backing and baste together (see page 144). Using toning machine quilting thread quilt in the ditch along all the seams. Trim the quilt edges and attach the binding (see page 145).

**QUILT ASSEMBLY DIAGRAM**

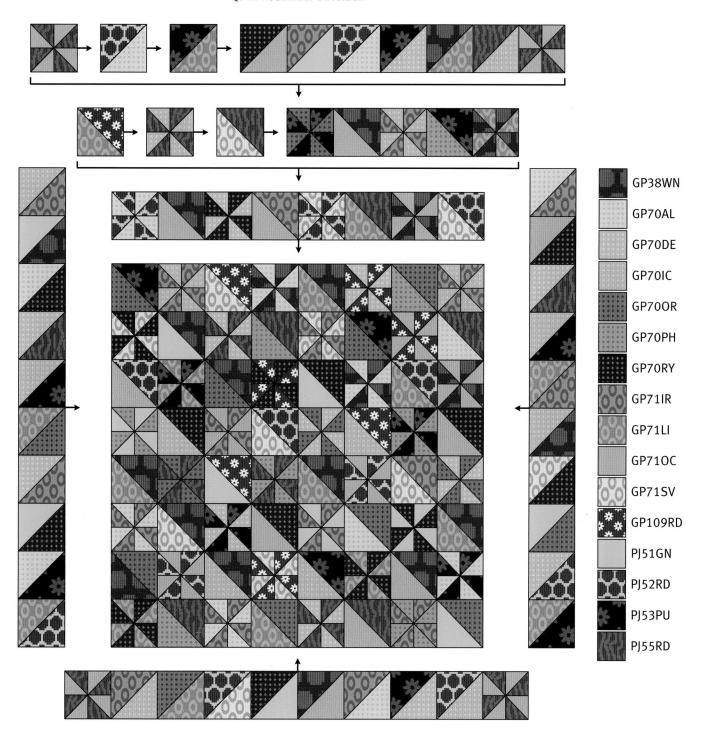

| | |
|---|---|
| | GP38WN |
| | GP70AL |
| | GP70DE |
| | GP70IC |
| | GP70OR |
| | GP70PH |
| | GP70RY |
| | GP71IR |
| | GP71LI |
| | GP71OC |
| | GP71SV |
| | GP109RD |
| | PJ51GN |
| | PJ52RD |
| | PJ53PU |
| | PJ55RD |

# amber snowball ***

## Kaffe Fassett

The centre of this quilt is made using traditional Snowball blocks, the shapes are an octagon and four triangles, in this case it is made 'the easy way' by using a large square (Template GG) and 4 small squares (Template HH) for each block. The small squares are placed over the corners of the large squares and stitched diagonally. They are then trimmed and flipped back to replace the corners of the large square. The placement of the corner triangles forms an interesting diamond pattern through the quilt. The Snowball blocks are combined in fours to make a larger block which finish at 6in (15.25cm). These blocks are set in straight rows and surrounded by a pieced border of 4-patch blocks made using the same large square (Template GG)

## SIZE OF QUILT
The finished quilt will measure approx. 78in x 90in (198cm x 228.5cm).

## MATERIALS
### Patchwork and Border Fabrics
RINGS
| Pink | BM15PK | ½yd (45cm) |
| Taupe | BM15TA | ⅜yd (35cm) |

ROMAN GLASS
| Blue & White | GP01BW | ⅜yd (35cm) |
| Dusty Pink | GP01DP | ½yd (45cm) |

PAPERWEIGHT
| Paprika | GP20PP | ¼yd (25cm) |

GUINEA FLOWER
| Blue | GP59BL | ⅜yd (35cm) |

SPOT
| China Blue | GP70CI | ¾yd (70cm) |
| Gold | GP70GD | ⅜yd (35cm) |
| Turquoise | GP70TQ | ¼yd (25cm) |

ABORIGINAL DOTS
| Cantaloupe | GP71CA | ½yd (45cm) |
| Gold | GP71GD | ⅞yd (80cm) |
| Lilac | GP71LI | ⅝yd (60cm) |
| Purple | GP71PU | 1yd (90cm) |

ASIAN CIRCLES
| Turquoise | GP89TQ | ½yd (45cm) |

MILLEFIORE
| Orange | GP92OR | ⅝yd (60cm) |

PLINK
| Lavender | GP109LV | ⅝yd (60cm) |

BABA GANOUSH
| Pink | GP124PK | ⅛yd (15cm) |
| Yellow | GP124YE | ⅝yd (60cm) |

TILE FLOWERS
| Turquoise | GP125TQ | ½yd (45cm) |

FRILLY
| Red | GP126RD | ⅜yd (35cm) |

CAMELLIA
| Pink | GP132PK | ¼yd (25cm) |

BRASSICA
| Brown | PJ51BR | ⅜yd (35cm) |

PICOTTE POPPIES
| Ochre | PJ52OC | ⅜yd (35cm) |

SHOT COTTON
| Scarlet | SC44 | ⅝yd (60cm) |
| Moor | SC52 | ¼yd (25cm) |
| Bronze | SC69 | ⅞yd (80cm) |

WOVEN ALTERNATE STRIPE
| Orange | WAS OR | ¼yd (45cm) |

**Backing Fabric** 6½yd (6m)
We suggest these fabrics for backing
BRASSICA Brown, PJ51BR
MILLEFIORE Orange, GP92OR
RINGS Taupe, BM15TA

**Binding**
SPOT
| Orange | GP70OR | ¾yd (70cm) |

**Batting**
86in x 98in (218.5cm x 249cm)

**Quilting thread**
Toning machine quilting thread

**Templates**

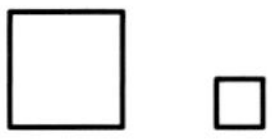

GG    HH

## CUTTING OUT
**Template GG** First fussy cut 4 squares 3½in x 3½in (9cm x 9cm) in WAS OR with the stripes aligned with the diagonal of the squares. For the remaining squares cut 3½in (9cm) strips across the width of the fabric. Each strip will give you 11 squares per full width. Cut 60 in GP70CI, 52 in GP71GD, GP92OR, GP124YE, 48 in GP109LV, 44 in GP89TQ, 40 in BM15PK, GP71PU, GP125TQ, 36 in GP01DP, 32 in BM15TA, GP126RD, SC44, 28 in GP59BL, GP70GD, PJ51BR, 24 in GP01BW, PJ52OC, 16 in GP20PP, GP71CA, GP132PK, WAS OR, 12 in GP70TQ and 8 in GP124PK. Total 780 squares.
**Template HH** Cut 1¼in (3.25cm) strips across the width of the fabric. Each strip will give you 32 squares per full width.

Cut 680 in SC69, 424 in GP71PU, 400 in GP71LI, 272 in GP71GD, 208 in SC44, 160 in GP71CA and 144 in SC52. Total 2288 squares.

**Binding** Cut 9 strips 2½in (6.5cm) across the width of the fabric in GP70OR.

**Backing** Cut 2 pieces 40in x 98in (101.5cm x 249), 2 pieces 40in x 7in (101.5cm x 17.75cm) and 1 piece 19in x 7in (48.25cm x 17.75cm) in backing fabric.

## MAKING THE BLOCKS
Use a ¼in (6mm) seam allowance throughout. We recommend using a design wall for this project. The layout of the template GG squares is shown clearly in the quilt assembly diagram, but as the corner triangles (Template HH squares) are so small we have provided a secondary diagram on a larger scale of the top left quadrant of the quilt showing just the corner squares to help with placement. The pattern is repeated in all 4 quadrants by mirroring the design.

We recommend starting with centre blocks and working out towards the quilt edge. The snowball blocks are pieced as shown in block assembly diagrams a and b, the finished block is shown in diagram c. Note that the corner fabric selection will vary depending on the position of the block within the quilt. Combine 4 snowball blocks as shown in diagram d to form the larger blocks which can be seen in diagram e. Make a total of 143 large blocks for the quilt centre.

Also piece the border 4-patch blocks using the remaining template GG squares as shown in diagrams f and g. Make 52 border blocks.

## MAKING THE QUILT
Piece the blocks into 13 rows of 11 blocks, join the rows to complete the quilt centre. Join the border blocks into 4 rows of 13 blocks each as shown in the quilt assembly diagram. Add the side borders followed by the top and bottom borders to complete the quilt.

# BLOCK ASSEMBLY DIAGRAMS

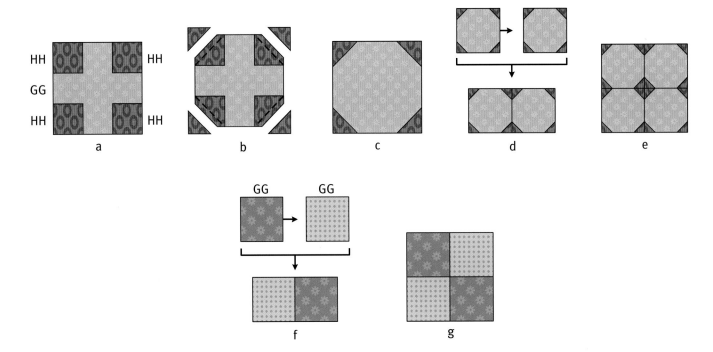

## CORNER TRIANGLES LAYOUT (TOP LEFT CORNER OF QUILT)

GP71CA

GP71GD

GP71LI

GP71PU

SC44

SC52

SC69

**FINISHING THE QUILT**

Press the quilt top. Seam the backing pieces using a ¼in (6mm) seam allowance to form a piece approx. 86in x 98in (218.5cm x 249cm). Layer the quilt top, batting and backing and baste together (see page 144). Using toning machine quilting thread stitch in the ditch in all the vertical and horizontal seams. Trim the quilt edges and attach the binding (see page 145).

# QUILT ASSEMBLY DIAGRAM

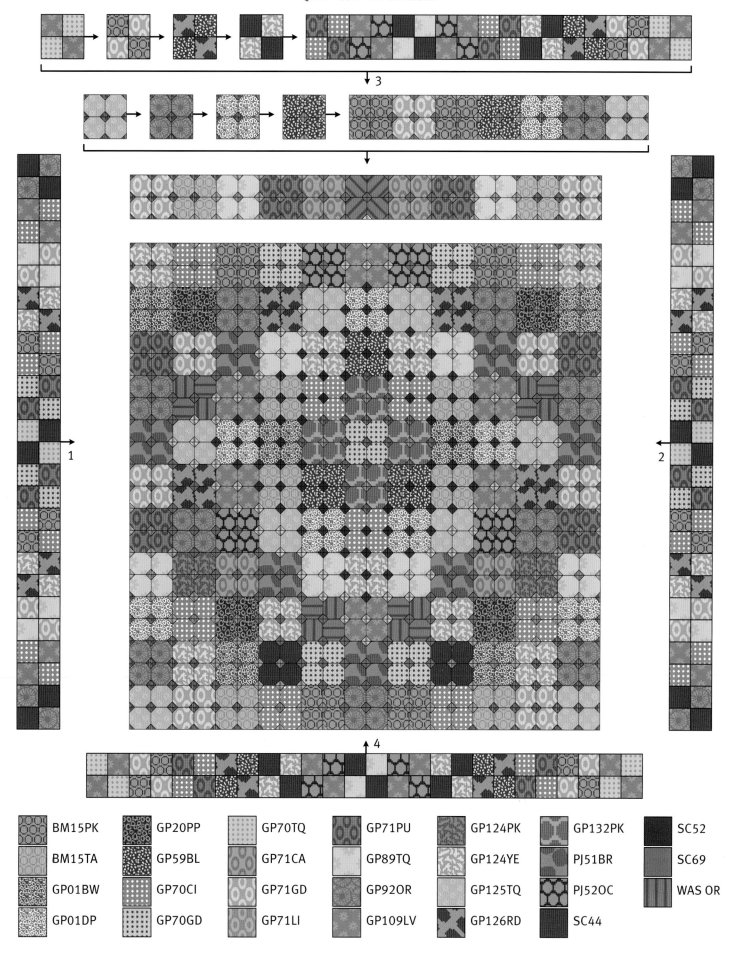

| BM15PK | GP20PP | GP70TQ | GP71PU | GP124PK | GP132PK | SC52 |
| BM15TA | GP59BL | GP71CA | GP89TQ | GP124YE | PJ51BR | SC69 |
| GP01BW | GP70CI | GP71GD | GP92OR | GP125TQ | PJ52OC | WAS OR |
| GP01DP | GP70GD | GP71LI | GP109LV | GP126RD | SC44 | |

# espania **

## Kaffe Fassett

All the shapes for this quilt are cut to size and no templates are provided for this design. Four panels make up the centre of this bold quilt, each is framed using strips and corner posts. The framed panels are separated by wide sashing with a centre post. The centre section is then surrounded with a simple border followed by a wider outer border with corner posts to complete the quilt.

## SIZE OF QUILT
The finished quilt will measure approx. 80½in x 98½in (204.5cm x 250.25cm).

## MATERIALS
**Patchwork and Border Fabrics**
OMBRE
| | | |
|---|---|---|
| Brown | GP117BR | 1yd (90cm) |

PETUNIAS
| | | |
|---|---|---|
| Ochre | PJ50OC | 1½yd (1.4m) |

GRANDIFLORA
| | | |
|---|---|---|
| Gold | PJ53GD | 1yd (90cm) |
| Old Rose | PJ53RO | 1yd (90cm) |
| Tomato | PJ53TM | 1yd (90cm) |

CACTUS DAHLIAS
| | | |
|---|---|---|
| Gold | PJ54GD | ¾yd (70cm) |

FEATHERS
| | | |
|---|---|---|
| Brown | PJ55BR | 2½yd (2.3m) |

WOVEN CATERPILLAR STRIPE
| | | |
|---|---|---|
| Yellow | WCS YE | 1¼yd (1.15m) |

**Backing Fabric** 7⅛yd (6.5m)
We suggest these fabrics for backing
MILLEFIORE Orange, GP92OR
PETUNIAS Ochre, PJ50OC
CACTUS DAHLIAS Gold, PJ54GD

**Binding**
JUPITER
| | | |
|---|---|---|
| Red | GP131RD | ⅞yd (80cm) |

**Batting**
88in x 106in (223.5cm x 269.25cm)

**Quilting thread**
Dark red machine quilting thread and deep pink perlé embroidery thread

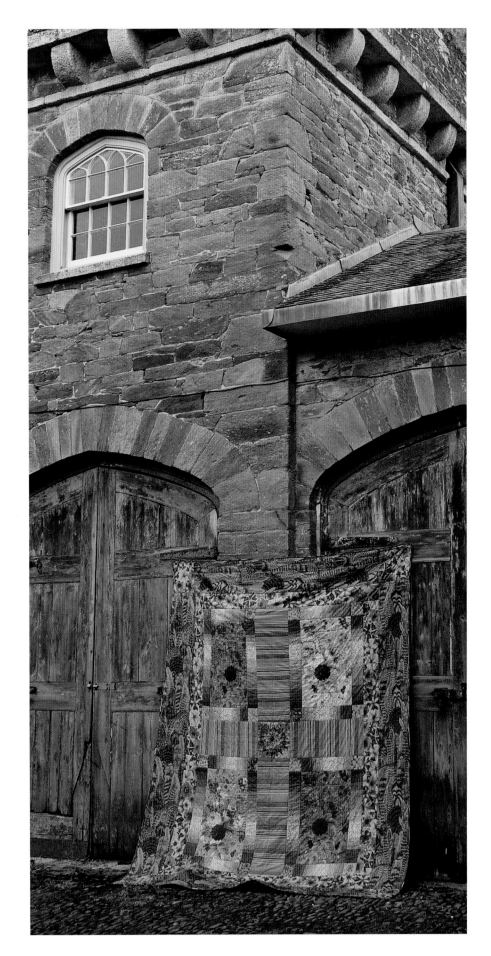

## CUTTING OUT

Cut the fabric in the order stated. Reserve remaining fabrics and use for later pieces as necessary.

**Piece A** Centring on the large floral sprays as shown in the photograph cut 2 panels 15in x 24in (38cm x 61cm) in PJ53TM, 1 in PJ53GD and PJ53RO. Total 4 panels.

**Piece B and C** Cut 8 strips 4in (10.25cm) wide across the width of the fabric. From each strip cut 1 piece 4in x 24in (10.25cm x 61cm) and 1 piece 4in x 15in (10.25cm x 38cm). Total 8 Piece B and 8 Piece C.

**Piece G** Cut 1 square 10in x 10in (25.5cm x 25.5cm) in PJ54GD for the sashing centre post (Fussy cut this square centring on a large bloom) and 4 in PJ50OC for the outer border corner posts.

**Piece D** Cut 16 squares 4in x 4in (10.25cm x 10.25cm) in PJ54GD

**Piece E and F** Cut 10in (25.5cm) strips across the width of the fabric, from these cut 2 vertical sashing strips 10in x 31in (25.5cm x 78.75cm) and 2 horizontal sashing strips 10in x 22in (25.5cm x 56cm) in WCS YE.

**Inner Borders** Cut 7 strips 5in (12.75cm) wide across the width of the fabric, join as necessary and cut 2 side inner borders 5in x 71in (12.75cm x 180.25cm) and 2 top and bottom inner borders 5in x 62in (12.75cm x 157.5cm) in PJ50OC.

**Outer Borders** Down the length of the fabric cut 2 side outer borders 10in x 80in (25.5cm x 203.25cm) and 2 top and bottom outer borders 10in x 62in (25.5cm x 157.5cm) in PJ55BR.

**Binding** Cut 10 strips 2½in (6.5cm) wide across the width of the fabric in GP131RD.

**Backing** Cut 2 pieces 40in x 106in (101.5cm x 269.25cm), 2 pieces 40in x 9in (101.5 x 22.75cm) and 1 piece 27in x 9in (68.5cm x 22.75cm) in backing fabric.

## MAKING THE QUILT CENTRE

Use a ¼in (6mm) seam allowance throughout. Refer to the quilt assembly diagram for fabric placement. Take the 4 centre panels and add the frames, starting with the sides as shown in centre panel assembly diagram a. Add a corner post to each end of the top and bottom strips and add to the centre panels.

## CENTRE PANEL ASSEMBLY DIAGRAMS

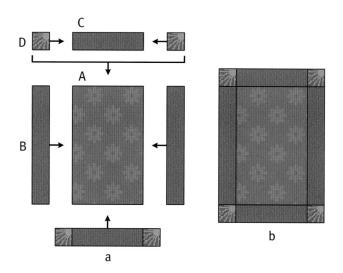

a

b

## HAND QUILTING DIAGRAM

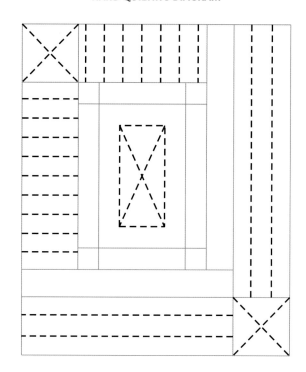

# QUILT ASSEMBLY DIAGRAM

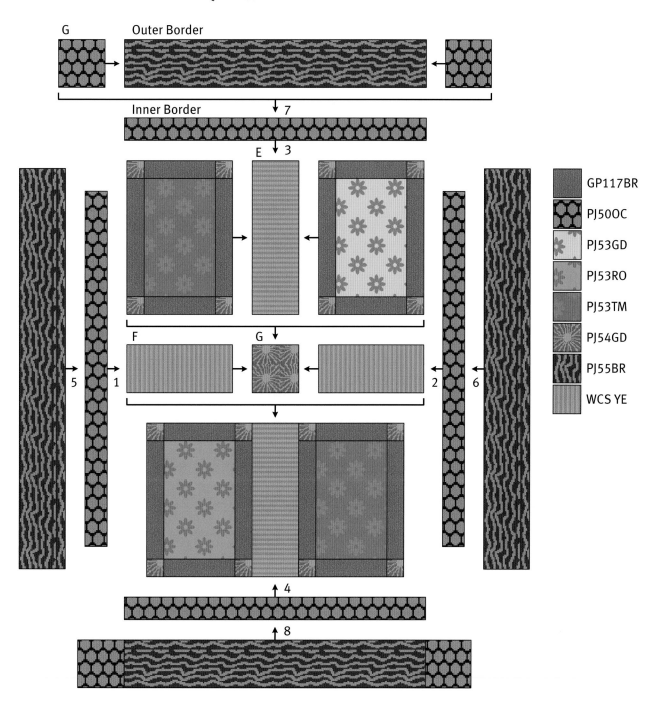

The finished centre panel is shown in diagram b.
Lay out the centre panels with the sashing as shown in the quilt assembly diagram, join to form 3 rows then join the rows to form the quilt centre.

## ADDING THE BORDERS
Join the side then top and bottom inner borders to the quilt centre as shown in

the quilt assembly diagram. Add the side outer borders to the quilt centre. Join an outer border corner post to each end of the top and bottom out borders and add to the quilt centre to complete the quilt.

## FINISHING THE QUILT
Press the quilt top. Seam the backing pieces using a ¼in (6mm) seam allowance to form a piece approx 88in x

106in (223.5cm x 269.25cm). Layer the quilt top, batting and backing and baste together (see page 144). Machine quilt in the ditch in all the seams using dark red machine quilting thread then hand quilt as shown in the hand quilting diagram using deep pink perlé embroidery thread. Trim the quilt edges and attach the binding (see page 145).

67

# overlapping squares **

### Kaffe Fassett

The illusion of overlapping squares in the blocks for this quilt is created using just 2 triangles (Templates G and Z). The bright print fabrics are set against a cool shot cotton background in blocks which finish to 12in (30.5cm) square and are set into straight rows. The quilt is framed with a simple border.

## SIZE OF QUILT
The finished quilt will measure approx. 59in x 71in (150cm x 180.25cm).

## MATERIALS
### Patchwork and Border Fabrics
DAISY CHAIN
| | | |
|---|---|---|
| Ochre | BM34OC | ¼yd (25cm) |
| Yellow | BM34YE | ¼yd (25cm) |

LOTTO
| | | |
|---|---|---|
| Grey | BM35GY | ¼yd (25cm) |
| Lilac | BM35LI | ¼yd (25cm) |

ASIAN CIRCLES
| | | |
|---|---|---|
| Turquoise | GP89TQ | ¼yd (25cm) |

OMBRE
| | | |
|---|---|---|
| Purple | GP117PU | ¼yd (25cm) |

ORIENTAL TREES
| | | |
|---|---|---|
| Brown | GP129BR | ¼yd (25cm) |
| Magenta | GP129MG | ¼yd (25cm) |
| Stone | GP129ST | ¼yd (25cm) |

PEKING
| | | |
|---|---|---|
| Pink | GP130PK | ¼yd (25cm) |
| Rust | GP130RU | ¼yd (25cm) |

JUPITER
| | | |
|---|---|---|
| Brown | GP131BR | ¼yd (25cm) |
| Purple | GP131PU | ¼yd (25cm) |
| Stone | GP131ST | 1¼yd (1.15m) |

GRANDIOSE
| | | |
|---|---|---|
| Grey | PJ13GY | ¼yd (25cm) |

BEGONIA LEAVES
| | | |
|---|---|---|
| Green | PJ18GN | ¼yd (25cm) |
| Grey | PJ18GY | ¼yd (25cm) |

FLOATING MUMS
| | | |
|---|---|---|
| Magenta | PJ56MG | ¼yd (25cm) |

SHOT COTTON
| | | |
|---|---|---|
| Aqua | SC77 | 1¼yd (1.15m) |

**Backing Fabric** 4yd (3.7m)
We suggest these fabrics for backing
FLOATING MUMS Duck Egg, PJ56DE
ORIENTAL TREES Stone, GP129ST
PEKING Pink, GP130PK

## Binding
SAND DOLLARS
| | | |
|---|---|---|
| Pastel | BM31PT | ⅞yd (60cm) |

## Batting
67in x 79in (170.25cm x 200.5cm)

## Quilting thread
Toning perlé embroidery threads

## Templates

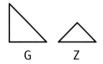

G    Z

## CUTTING OUT
Cut the fabric in the order stated to prevent waste.

**Background Fabric SC77 only**

**Template Z** Cut 5¼in (13.5cm) strips across the width of the fabric. Each strip will give you 28 triangles per full width. From the strips cut 5¼in (13.5cm) squares then cut each square twice diagonally to make 4 triangles using the template as a guide, do not move the patches until both diagonals have been cut. This will ensure the long side of the triangle will not have a bias edge. Cut 80 in SC77.

**Template G** Cut 4⅞in (12.5cm) strips across the width of the fabric, Each strip will give you 16 triangles per full width. Cut 4⅞in (12.5cm) squares, then cut each square diagonally to form 2 triangles using the template as a guide. Handle the triangles carefully as the long edge will be on the bias and stretchy. Cut 80 in SC77.

**Print Fabrics**

**Borders** Cut 6 strips 6in (15.25cm) wide across the width of the fabric. Join as necessary and cut 2 borders 6in x 60½in (15.25cm x 153.75cm) for the quilt sides and 2 borders 6in x 59½in (15.25cm x 151.25cm) for the quilt top and bottom in GP131ST.

**Template Z** Cut a 5¼in (13.5cm) strip across the width of the fabric. From the strip cut 5¼in (13.5cm) squares (only cut the number required to ensure you will have enough fabric for later templates). Cut each square twice diagonally to make 4 triangles using the template as a guide, do not move the patches until both diagonals have been cut. This will ensure the long side of the triangle will not have a bias edge. Cut 10 triangles in BM35GY, BM35LI. GP89TQ, GP129MG, GP130PK, GP130RU. GP131BR, GP131PU, GP131ST, PJ13GY, PJ18GY, PJ56MG, 8 in BM34YE, GP117PU, GP129BR, GP129ST, 4 in BM34OC and PJ18GN. Total 160 triangles. Reserve the leftover strip and trim for Template G.

**Template G** Trim the leftover strip from template Z to 4⅞in (12.5cm). Cut 4⅞in (12.5cm) squares, then cut each square diagonally to form 2 triangles using the template as a guide. Handle the triangles carefully as the long edge will be on the bias and stretchy. Cut 10 triangles in BM35GY, BM35LI. GP89TQ, GP129MG, GP130PK, GP130RU. GP131BR, GP131PU, GP131ST, PJ13GY, PJ18GY, PJ56MG, 8 in BM34YE, GP117PU, GP129BR, GP129ST, 4 in BM34OC and PJ18GN. Total 160 triangles.

**Binding** Cut 7 strips 2½in (6.5cm) wide across the width of the fabric in BM31PT.

**Backing** Cut 2 pieces 40in x 67in (101.5cm x 170.25cm) in backing fabric.

## MAKING THE BLOCKS
Use a ¼in (6mm) seam allowance throughout. Refer to the quilt assembly diagram for fabric placement. In some cases the wrong side of the fabric was used as Kaffe wanted a softer look, we have marked the quilt assembly diagram with small white circles to show the position of these fabrics.

There are 3 types of unit in each block, the first uses 2 template G triangles, the second uses 1 template G triangle and 2 template Z triangles and the third 4 template Z triangles. For each block make 4 units as shown in block assembly diagram a, the finished unit is shown in diagram b. Next make 4 units as shown in diagram c and d, the finished unit is shown in diagram e. Finally make 1 unit as shown in diagram f and g, the finished unit is shown in diagram h. Arrange the 9 units as shown in diagram i and piece into 3 rows, join the rows as shown in diagram j. The finished block can be seen in diagram k. Make 20 blocks.

## BLOCK ASSEMBLY DIAGRAMS

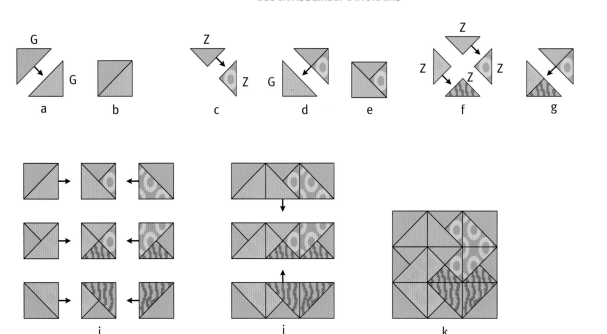

a  b  c  d  e  f  g  h

i  j  k

## QUILTING DIAGRAM

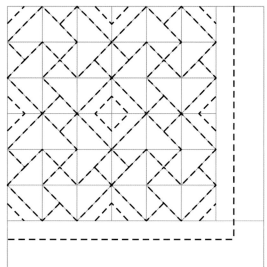

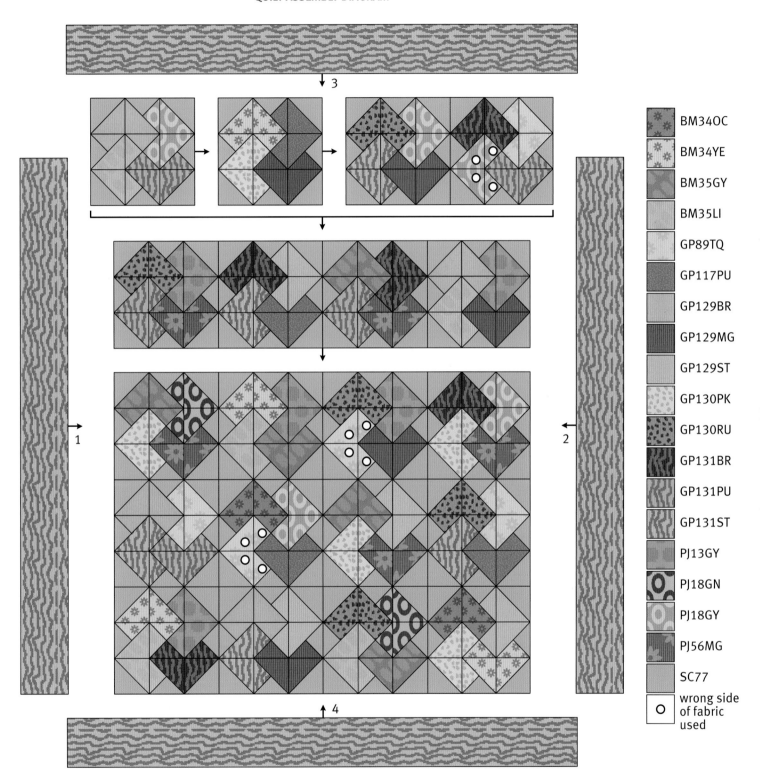

BM34OC
BM34YE
BM35GY
BM35LI
GP89TQ
GP117PU
GP129BR
GP129MG
GP129ST
GP130PK
GP130RU
GP131BR
GP131PU
GP131ST
PJ13GY
PJ18GN
PJ18GY
PJ56MG
SC77
wrong side of fabric used

## MAKING THE QUILT

Lay out the blocks into 5 rows of 4 blocks, join the rows to complete the quilt centre. Join the side borders to the quilt centre, followed by the top and bottom borders as shown in the quilt assembly diagram.

## FINISHING THE QUILT

Press the quilt top. Seam the backing pieces using a ¼in (6mm) seam allowance to form a piece approx. 67in x 79in (170.25cm x 200.5cm). Layer the quilt top, batting and backing and baste together (see page 144). Using toning perlé embroidery threads hand quilt as shown in the quilting diagram. Trim the quilt edges and attach the binding (see page 145).

# misty log cabin **

Kaffe Fassett

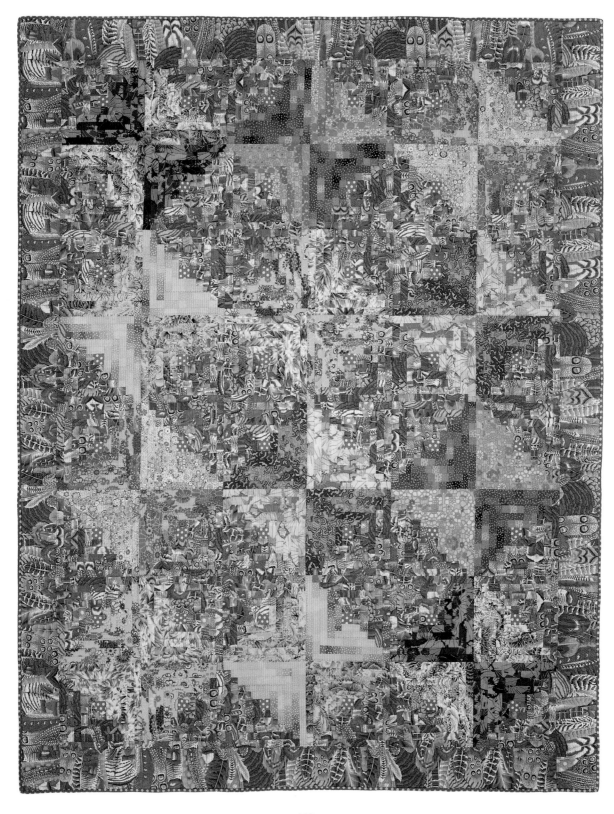

All the fabric for this quilt is cut to size and no templates are provided. Kaffe chose Philip Jacobs' Feather fabric as the main ingredient of this quilt and added a selection of 12 contrasting prints in soft shades. The log cabin blocks are set into straight rows and the quilt is completed with a simple border.

## SIZE OF QUILT
The finished quilt will measure approx. 80in x 103in (203.25cm x 261.5cm).

## MATERIALS
### Patchwork and Border Fabrics

| LOTUS LEAF | | |
|---|---|---|
| Antique | GP29AN | ½yd (45cm) |
| Jade | GP29JA | ½yd (45cm) |
| SPOT | | |
| Teal | GP70TE | ¼yd (25cm) |
| ASIAN CIRCLES | | |
| Green | GP89GN | ½yd (45cm) |
| Turquoise | GP89TQ | ½yd (45cm) |
| MILLEFIORE | | |
| Lilac | GP92LI | ½yd (45cm) |
| OMBRE | | |
| Moss | GP117MS | ½yd (45cm) |
| Purple | GP117PU | ½yd (45cm) |
| BABA GANOUSH | | |
| Umber | GP124UM | ½yd (45cm) |
| TILE FLOWERS | | |
| Turquoise | GP125TQ | ½yd (45cm) |
| BRASSICA | | |
| Green | PJ51GN | ½yd (45cm) |
| Pastel | PJ51PT | ½yd (45cm) |
| CACTUS DAHLIAS | | |
| Pastel | PJ54PT | ½yd (45cm) |
| FEATHERS | | |
| Grey | PJ55GY | 6yd (5.5m) |

**Backing Fabric** 7⅜yd (6.7m)
We suggest these fabrics for backing
FEATHERS Soft, PJ55SF
BABA GANOUSH Umber, GP124UM
BRASSICA Grey, PJ51GY

### Binding
SPOT
Grape      GP70GP      ⅞yd (80cm)

### Batting
88in x 111in (223.5cm x 282cm)

### Quilting thread
Lavender perlé embroidery thread

## CUTTING OUT
Cut the fabric as stated to ensure you have sufficient of each fabric.
**Borders** Cut 9 strips 6in (15.25cm) wide across the width of the fabric in PJ55GY. Join the strips as necessary and cut 2 borders 6in x 103½in (15.25cm x 263cm) for the quilt sides and 2 borders 6in x 69½in (15.25cm x 176.5cm) for the quilt top and bottom.
**Log Cabin Centres** Cut 2in (5cm) strips across the width of the fabric, each strip will give you 20 squares. Cut 48 squares 2in x 2in (5cm x 5cm) in GP70TE.
**Log Cabin Strips** Each block is made using Feathers PJ55GY and a contrasting fabric. It takes 2 strips of each to complete the block. Cut 1½in (3.75cm) strips across the width of the fabric. Cut 96 strips in PJ55GY, 8 strips in each of the contrast fabrics, GP29AN, GP29JA, GP89GN, GP89TQ, GP92LI, GP117MS, GP117PU, GP124UM, GP125TQ, PJ51GN, PJ51PT and PJ54PT.

Log Sizes refer to the block diagram
Log 1   1½in x 2in (3.75 x 5cm) in PJ55GY
Log 2   1½in x 3in (3.75 x 7.5cm) in PJ55GY
Log 3   1½in x 3in (3.75 x 7.5cm) in contrast fabric
Log 4   1½in x 4in (3.75 x 10.25cm) in contrast fabric
Log 5   1½in x 4in (3.75 x 10.25cm) in PJ55GY
Log 6   1½in x 5in (3.75 x 12.75cm) in PJ55GY
Log 7   1½in x 5in (3.75 x 12.75cm) in contrast fabric
Log 8   1½in x 6in (3.75 x 15.25cm) in contrast fabric
Log 9   1½in x 6in (3.75 x 15.25cm) in PJ55GY
Log 10  1½in x 7in (3.75 x 17.75cm) in PJ55GY
Log 11  1½in x 7in (3.75 x 17.75cm) in contrast fabric
Log 12  1½in x 8in (3.75 x 20.25cm) in contrast fabric
Log 13  1½in x 8in (3.75 x 20.25cm) in PJ55GY
Log 14  1½in x 9in (3.75 x 22.75cm) in PJ55GY
Log 15  1½in x 9in (3.75 x 22.75cm) in contrast fabric
Log 16  1½in x 10in (3.75 x 25.5cm) in contrast fabric
Log 17  1½in x 10in (3.75 x 25.5cm) in PJ55GY
Log 18  1½in x 11in (3.75 x 28cm) in PJ55GY
Log 19  1½in x 11in (3.75 x 28cm) in contrast fabric
Log 20  1½in x 12in (3.75 x 30.5cm) in contrast fabric

Cut logs 1, 2, 5, 6, 9, 10 and 13 from the first strip of PJ55GY
Cut logs 14, 17 and 18 from the second strip of PJ55GY
Cut logs 3, 4, 7, 11, 12 and 15 from the first strip of contrast fabric
Cut logs 8, 16, 19 and 20 from the second strip of contrast fabric

**Binding** Cut 10 strips 2½in (6.5cm) wide across the width of the fabric in GP70GP.

**Backing** Cut 2 pieces 40in x 111in (101.5cm x 282cm), 2 pieces 40in x 9in (101.5 x 23cm) and 1 piece 32in x 9in (81.25cm x 23cm) in backing fabric.

### Kaffe says:

An accurate ¼in (6mm) seam allowance is essential when sewing log cabin blocks, a tiny deviation from this allowance can make your blocks too large or too small so check your machine is set correctly.

**BLOCK DIAGRAM**

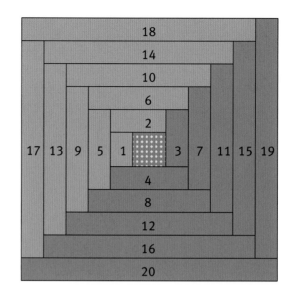

**BLOCK ASSEMBLY DIAGRAMS**

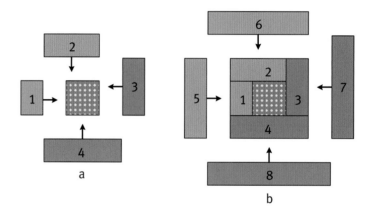

a

b

### MAKING THE BLOCKS

Use a ¼in (6mm) seam allowance throughout. Refer to the quilt assembly diagram for fabric placement. Take a centre square and add the first 4 logs in numerical order as shown in block assembly diagram a. Take the next 4 logs and add to the block centre as shown in diagram b. Continue to add logs in numerical order until the block is complete as shown in the block diagram. Make 48 blocks.

### MAKING THE QUILT

Lay out the blocks as shown in the quilt assembly diagram and stitch into 8 rows of 6 blocks. Join the rows to form the quilt centre. Add the top and bottom borders followed by the side borders to complete the quilt.

### FINISHING THE QUILT

Press the quilt top. Seam the backing pieces using a ¼in (6mm) seam allowance to form a piece approx. 88in x·111in (223.5cm x 282cm). Layer the quilt top, batting and backing and baste together (see page 144). Hand quilt ¼in (6mm) offset from the seams between the blocks and ¼in (6mm) inside the outer seam line of the second round of logs (which makes an approx. 5in (12.75cm square) in lavender perlé embroidery thread. Trim the quilt edges and attach the binding (see page 145).

# QUILT ASSEMBLY DIAGRAM

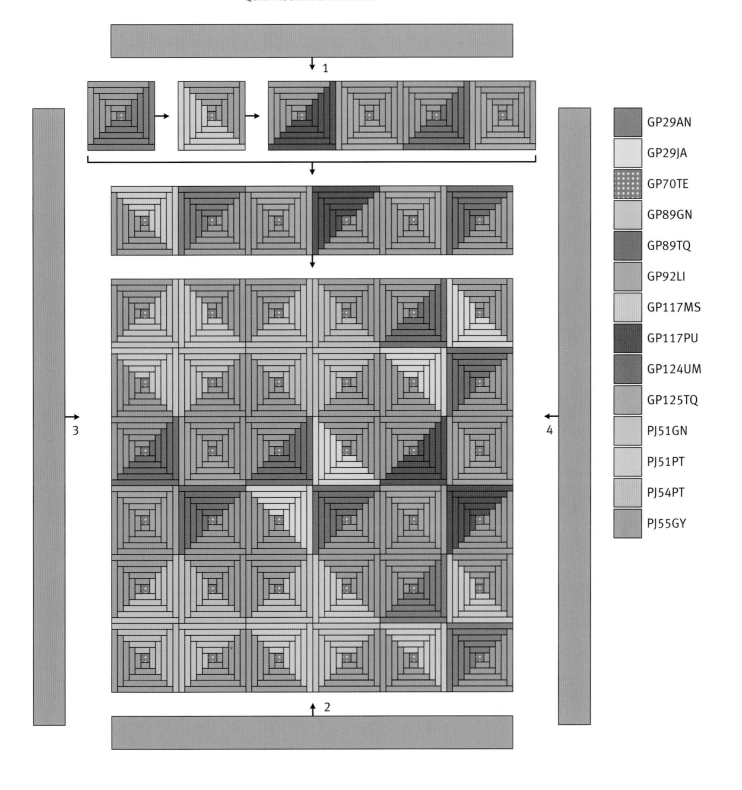

GP29AN
GP29JA
GP70TE
GP89GN
GP89TQ
GP92LI
GP117MS
GP117PU
GP124UM
GP125TQ
PJ51GN
PJ51PT
PJ54PT
PJ55GY

# rick rack ✱✱✱

## Kaffe Fassett

The centre of this striking quilt is made using a square (Template S) and a triangle (Template T) which are pieced into rows. The ends of some rows are completed with a second triangle (Template U). The quilt centre is surrounded with a pieced border made using a rectangle (Template V) and a triangle (Template T again). The borders are trimmed off to fit and have pieced corner posts made using a square (Template W) and 2 rectangles (Templates X and Y) which are used to frame the square.

## SIZE OF QUILT
The finished quilt will measure approx. 75in x 94in (190.5cm x 238.75cm).

## MATERIALS
**Patchwork and Border Fabrics**
GUINEA FLOWER
| Pink | GP59PK | ⅝yd 60cm |

ABORIGINAL DOTS
| Lime | GP71LM | ½yd (45cm) |
| Ocean | GP71ON | ¾yd (70cm) |

PLINK
| Lavender | GP109LV | ½yd (45cm) |
| Turquoise | GP109TQ | ⅝yd (60cm) |

PICOTTE POPPIES
| Turquoise | PJ52TQ | ⅜yd (35cm) |

SHOT COTTON
| Thunder | SC06 | 1⅜yd (1.25m) |
| Raspberry | SC08 | ¼yd (25cm) |
| Chartreuse | SC12 | ¼yd (25cm) |
| Lavender | SC14 | ¼yd (25cm) |
| Jade | SC41 | ½yd (45cm) |
| Lime | SC43 | ⅞yd (80cm) |
| Aegean | SC46 | 2⅜yd (2.2m) |
| Cactus | SC92 | ⅝yd (60cm) |

**Backing Fabric** 6½yd (5.9m)
We suggest these fabrics for backing
JAPANESE CRYSANTHEMUM Purple, PJ41PU
ABORIGINAL DOTS Ocean, GP71ON
PLINK Lavender, GP109LV

**Binding**
SPOT
| Black | GP70BK | ¾yd (70cm) |

**Batting**
83in x 102in (210.75cm x 259cm)

**Quilting thread**
Toning machine quilting thread

## Templates

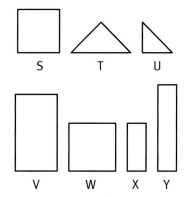

## CUTTING OUT
**Template S** Cut 5in (12.75cm) strips across the width of the fabric. Each strip will give you 8 squares per full width. Cut 93 in SC46.

**Template T** Cut 7⅝in (19.5cm) strips across the width of the fabric. Each strip will give you 20 triangles per full width. From the strips cut 7⅝in (19.5cm) squares, then cut each square twice diagonally to make 4 triangles using the template as a guide, do not move the patches until both diagonals have been cut. This will ensure the long side of the triangle will not have a bias edge. Cut 90 in SC06, 34 in SC43, 30 in SC46, 17 in GP59PK, GP71LM, GP71ON , GP109LV, GP109TQ, SC08, SC12, SC14, SC41 and SC92. Reserve leftover fabric for template U. Total 324 triangles.

**Template U** Cut 4⅛in (10.5cm) squares, then cut each square diagonally to form 2 triangles using the template as a guide. Cut 4 in SC43, 2 in GP59PK, GP71LM, GP71ON, GP109LV, GP109TQ, SC08, SC12, SC14, SC41 and SC92. Total 24 triangles.

**Template V** Cut 5in (12.75cm) strips across the width of the fabric. Each strip will give you 4 rectangles per full width. Cut 5in x 8½in (12.75cm x 21.5cm) rectangles, cut 8 in PJ52TQ, 7 in SC43, SC92, 6 in GP59PK, 5 in GP71ON, GP109TQ, 3 in GP71LM, GP109LV and 2 in SC41. Total 46 rectangles.

**Template W** Cut 5½in (14cm) squares. Cut 4 in SC06.

**Template X** Cut 2½in (6.5cm) strips across the width of the fabric. Each strip will give you 7 rectangles per full width. Cut 2½in x 5½in (6.5cm x 15cm) rectangles. Cut 8 in GP71ON.

**Template Y** Cut 2½in (6.5cm) strips across the width of the fabric. Each strip will give you 4 rectangles per full width. Cut 2½in x 9½in (6.5cm x 24.25cm) rectangles. Cut 8 in GP71ON.

## ROW ASSEMBLY DIAGRAM

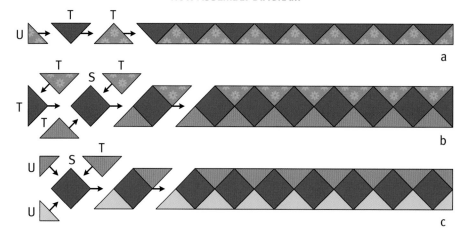

a

b

c

## BORDER ASSEMBLY DIAGRAM

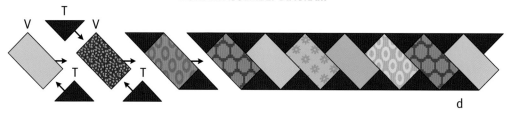

d

## BORDER CORNER POST ASSEMBLY DIAGRAM

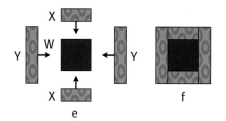

e

f

**Binding** Cut 9 strips 2½in (6.5cm) wide across the width of the fabric in GP70BK.

**Backing** Cut 2 pieces 40in x 102in (101.5cm x 259cm), 2 pieces 40in x 4in (101.5cm x 10cm) and 1 piece 23in x 4in (58.5cm x 10cm) in backing fabric.

### MAKING THE QUILT CENTRE
Use a ¼in (6mm) seam allowance throughout. Refer to the quilt assembly diagram for fabric placement. Piece the rows as shown in the row assembly diagrams. Diagram a shows the top (and bottom) row, diagram b the second row and diagram c the third row. The second and third rows are repeated alternately down the quilt centre then the bottom

row is a repeat of the top row. Join the rows to complete the quilt centre as shown in the quilt assembly diagram.

### MAKING THE BORDER
Piece the top border as shown in border assembly diagram d. The border will be longer than necessary as the ends will be trimmed to fit. Align the top border to the quilt centre matching the template T triangles to the top row, trim the border to fit (make sure you include a seam allowance). Make the other 3 borders in the same manner and trim each to fit the quilt centre. Make the 4 border corner posts as shown in border corner post assembly diagrams e and f.

### MAKING THE QUILT
Join the top and bottom borders to the quilt centre. Join a border corner post to each end of the side borders and add to the quilt centre to complete the quilt.

### FINISHING THE QUILT
Press the quilt top. Seam the backing pieces using a ¼in (6mm) seam allowance to form a piece approx. 83in x 102in (210.75cm x 259cm). Layer the quilt top, batting and backing and baste together (see page 144). Using toning machine quilting thread stitch in the ditch along all the seams with the exception of the horizontal seams between the rows in the quilt centre. Trim the quilt edges and attach the binding (see page 145).

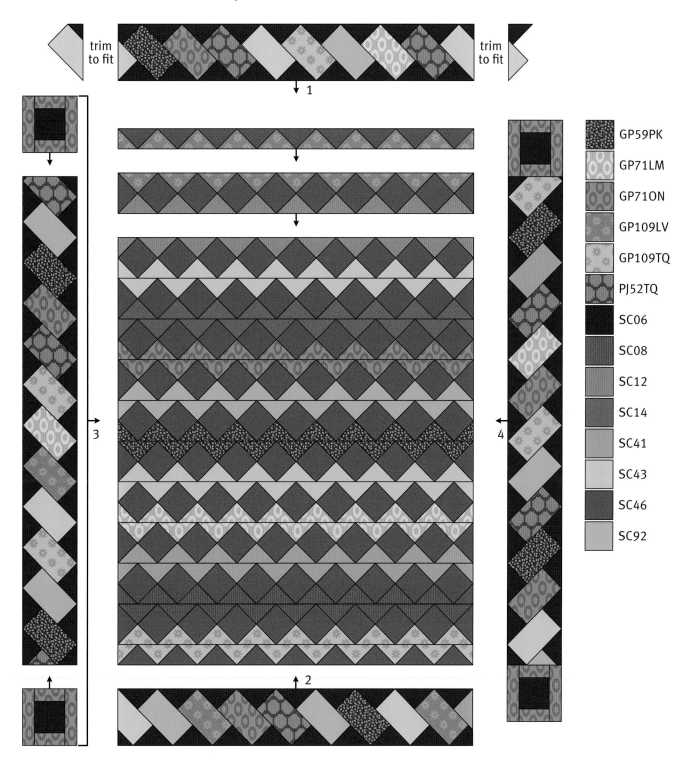

GP59PK
GP71LM
GP71ON
GP109LV
GP109TQ
PJ52TQ
SC06
SC08
SC12
SC14
SC41
SC43
SC46
SC92

# double diamond ***

### Kaffe Fassett

This pastel coloured quilt is made using a 60 degree diamond (Template AA) with 3 triangles (Templates BB, CC and DD & Reverse DD) used to provide partial diamond blocks along the quilt edges and corners. The diamonds are framed with 2 layers of strips which are cut to size as the quilt is pieced. Sashing strips (Template EE & Reverse EE) and diamond corner posts (Template FF) interspace the framed diamonds. The quilt is pieced in diagonal rows and completed with a simple border.

## SIZE OF QUILT
The finished quilt will measure approx. 75¾in x 93in (192.5cm x 236.25cm).

## MATERIALS
### Patchwork Fabrics
SAND DOLLARS
| Pastel | BM31PT | ¾yd (70cm) |
CABBAGE AND ROSE
| Spring | GP38SP | ⅜yd (35cm) |
GUINEA FLOWER
| Mauve | GP59MV | ⅞yd 80cm |
SPOT
| China Blue | GP70CI | ⅞yd (80cm) |
| Hydrangea | GP70HY | ⅝yd (60cm) |
| Lavender | GP70LV | ⅝yd (60cm) |
| Mint | GP70MT | ¾yd (70cm) |
| Peach | GP70PH | ⅝yd (60cm) |
| Sky Blue | GP70SK | ¾yd (70cm) |
PETUNIAS
| Pastel | PJ50PT | ½yd (45cm) |
PICOTTE POPPIES
| Pastel | PJ52PT | ½yd (45cm) |
CACTUS DAHLIAS
| Pastel | PJ54PT | ½yd (45cm) |
BANDED POPPY
| Mint | PJ59MT | ⅜yd (35cm) |
| Natural | PJ59NL | ⅜yd (35cm) |
| Peach | PJ59PH | ⅜yd (35cm) |

### Border and Sashing Fabric
SPOT
| Magnolia | GP70MN | 3yd (2.75m) |

### Backing Fabric 6½yd (5.9m)
We suggest these fabrics for backing
MILLEFIORE Pastel, GP92PT
PETUNIAS Pastel, PJ50PT
CACTUS DAHLIA Pastel, PJ54PT

### Binding
PETUNIAS
| Pastel | PJ50PT | ¾yd (70cm) |

### Batting
84in x 101in (213.25cm x 256.5cm)

### Quilting thread
Toning machine quilting thread

## Templates

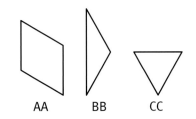

AA     BB     CC

DD
& reverse DD    EE & reverse EE    FF

## CUTTING OUT
Cut the fabric in the order stated to prevent waste and trim leftover strips for later shapes. Reserve all leftover fabrics in the largest piece possible. We have included a cutting layout for fabric GP70MN from which the borders, sashing and sashing corner posts are cut.

**Template CC** Cut 5¼in (13.25cm) across the width of the fabric. Each strip will give you 12 triangles per full width. Cut 4 in PJ54PT, 2 in PJ50PT, PJ59MT, 1 in GP38SP, PJ52PT, PJ59NL and PJ59PH. Total 12 triangles. Reserve leftover strips and trim for templates AA, BB and DD & reverse DD.
**Template AA** Cut 5in (12.75cm) strips across the width of the fabric. Each strip will give you 6 diamonds per full width. Cut 11 in PJ54PT, 10 in GP38SP, PJ50PT, 9 in PJ52PT, 7 in PJ59PH, 6 in PJ59MT and PJ59NL. Total 59 diamonds.
**Template DD & Reverse DD** Cut 1 in PJ59MT and 1 in PJ59PH. Reverse the template by flipping it over, cut 1 in PJ50PT and 1 in PJ59PH. Total 4 triangles.
**Template BB** Cut 3⅛in (8cm) strips across the width of the fabric. Each strip will give

you 6 triangles per full width. Cut 3 in PJ59MT, PJ59NL and 2 in PJ52PT. Total 8 triangles.
**Framing Strips** Cut 1¼in (3.25cm) strips across the width of the fabric. Cut 21 strips in GP59MV, 20 in GP70CI, 19 in GP70SK, 16 in BM31PT, GP70MT, 15 in GP70HY, 14 in GP70PH and 13 in GP70LV. The strips will be cut to length during the piecing process.
**Borders** Please refer to the cutting layout for GP70MN for this item. Down the length of the fabric cut 2 borders 2in x 92in (5cm x 233.75cm) for the quilt sides and 2 borders 2in x 78in (5cm x 198cm) for the quilt top and bottom in GP70MN. These are cut a little oversize and will be trimmed to fit later.
**Template EE & Reverse EE** Please refer to the cutting layout for GP70MN for this item. Cut 2in (5cm) strips down the length of the fabric as shown in the layout. Cut 70 sashing strips, then reverse the template by flipping it over and cut a further 70 sashing strips in GP70MN. Total 140 strips.

## CUTTING LAYOUT FOR GP70MN

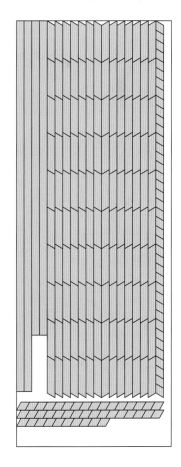

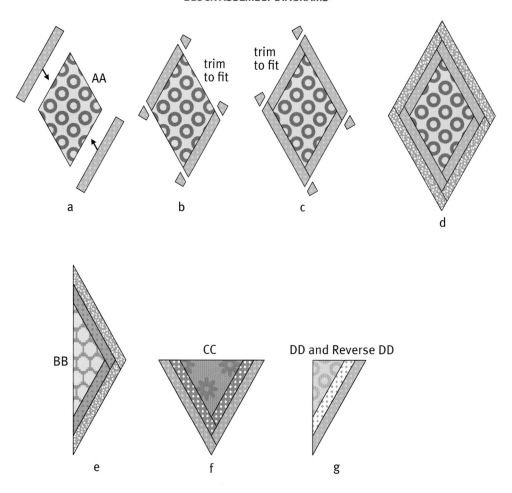

a

b

trim
to fit

trim
to fit

c

d

AA

BB

e

CC

f

DD and Reverse DD

g

**Template FF** Please refer to the cutting layout for GP70MN for this item. Cut 2in (5cm) strips as shown in the layout. Cut 82 diamonds in GP70MN.

**Binding** Cut 9 strips 2½in (6.5cm) wide across the width of the fabric in PJ50PT.

**Backing** Cut 2 pieces 40in x 101in (101.5cm x 256.5cm), 2 pieces 40in x 5in (101.5cm x 12.75cm) and 1 piece 22in x 5in (56cm x 12.75cm) in backing fabric.

**MAKING THE BLOCKS**
Use a ¼in (6mm) seam allowance throughout. Refer to the quilt assembly diagram for fabric placement. Take a template AA diamond and add a 1¼in (3.25cm) to each side as shown in block assembly diagram a. To speed this process you can piece several diamonds to strips at a time, but be careful to leave a gap between each so when the strip is pressed back it can be cut at an angle as shown in diagram b. Press the blocks and

trim the strips to fit the raw edge of the diamond. This can be done with a rotary cutter and ruler, or use a ruler and pencil to mark the angle and cut carefully with scissors. Repeat the process with the opposite sides and trim in the same way to complete the inner frame as shown in diagram c. Next add the outer frame in the same manner, the finished diamond block is shown in diagram d. Make a total of 59 blocks.

The edges of the quilt are filled with 3 triangle shapes, pieced in the same way with framing strips. The 8 side triangles are made using template BB triangles as shown in diagram e with framing strips along the 2 short sides. The 12 top and bottom triangles are made using template CC triangles as shown in diagram f with framing strips on 2 sides. The 4 corner triangles are made using template DD & Reverse DD triangles with framing strips only along the long side as shown in diagram g.

**MAKING THE QUILT**
Lay out the blocks interspaced with the template EE & Reverse EE sashing strips and template FF diamonds. Separate carefully into diagonal rows as shown in the quilt assembly diagram. Join the blocks and sashing into rows as shown, then join the rows. Trim the template FF diamonds flush with the raw edge to complete the quilt centre. Finally add the side borders and trim to fit then add the top and bottom borders and trim to complete the quilt.

**FINISHING THE QUILT**
Press the quilt top. Seam the backing pieces using a ¼in (6mm) seam allowance to form a piece approx. 84in x 101in (213.25cm x 256.5cm) Layer the quilt top, batting and backing and baste together (see page 144). Using toning machine quilting thread stitch in the ditch to outline each diamond, then in all the sashing seams. Trim the quilt edges and attach the binding (see page 145).

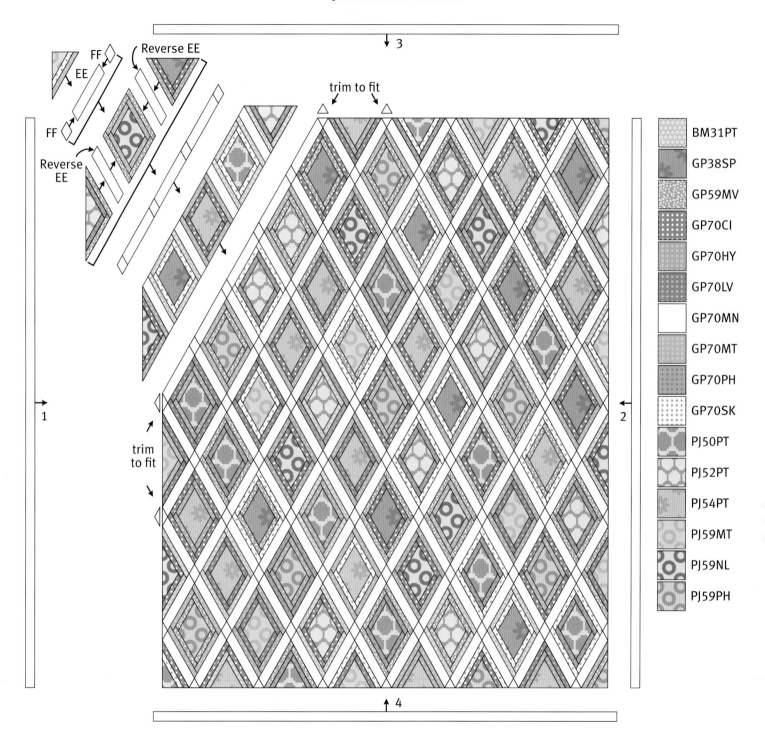

# mirror squares *

## Kaffe Fassett

The shapes for this quilt are cut to size and templates are not provided, however we suggest you make templates for the side and corner setting triangles to allow fussy cutting of the fabric (details on how to do this in the cutting instructions). Large squares (Large Square) are pieced into rows set 'on point' for this design. The edges of the quilt are filled using 2 triangles (Side Setting Triangle and Corner Setting Triangle). The placement of the fabrics is the key to this design, with the squares mirrored in both horizontal and vertical directions.

## SIZE OF QUILT
The finished quilt will measure approx. 94in x 94in (238.75cm x 238.75cm).

## MATERIALS
**Patchwork Fabrics**
AUGUST ROSE
Antique         GP18AN        ⅝yd (60cm)
CABBAGE AND ROSE
Fuchsia         GP38FU        ⅝yd (60cm)
BIG BLOOMS
Brown           GP91BR        ⅜yd (35cm)
BABA GANOUSH
Brown           GP124BR       ⅝yd (60cm)
TILE FLOWERS
Brown           GP125BR       ⅝yd (60cm)
FRILLY
Blue            GP126BL       ⅜yd (35cm)
Orange          GP126OR       ⅝yd (60cm)
Red             GP126RD       ⅝yd (60cm)
PARASOLS
Ochre           GP127OC       ⅝yd (60cm)
JAPANESE CHRYSANTHEMUM
Scarlet         GP41SC        ⅜yd (35cm)
BRASSICA
Red             GP51RD        ⅝yd (60cm)
GRANDIFLORA
Old Rose        PJ53RO        ⅝yd (60cm)
Tomato          PJ53TM        ⅝yd (60cm)
BANDED POPPY
Carmine         PJ59CM        ⅜yd (35cm)
WOVEN CATERPILLAR STRIPE
Yellow          WCS YE        1⅝yd (1.5m)

**Backing Fabric**  8⅛yd (7.4m)
We suggest these fabrics for backing
JAPANESE CHRYSANTHEMUM Scarlet, PJ41SC
CABBAGE AND ROSE Fuchsia, GP38FU
GRANDIFLORA Old Rose, PJ53RO

**Binding**
PARASOLS
Black           GP127BK       ⅞yd (80cm)

**Batting**
102in x 102in (259cm x 259cm)

**Quilting thread**
Toning machine quilting thread and toning perlé embroidery thread

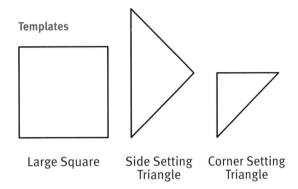

Templates

Large Square          Side Setting          Corner Setting
                      Triangle              Triangle

## CUTTING OUT
The setting triangles are fussy cut to align with the stripe direction of the Woven Caterpillar Stripe. We have provided a cutting layout for this fabric.
**Large Square** Cut 10in (25.5cm) strips across the width of the fabric. Each strip will give you 4 squares per full width. Cut 10in (25.5cm) squares. Cut 8 in GP38FU, GP125BR, GP127OC, PJ51RD, PJ53TM, 6 in GP18AN, GP124BR, GP126OR, GP126RD, 5 in PJ53RO, 4 in GP91BR, GP126BL, PJ41SC and PJ59CM. Total 85 squares.
**Side Setting Triangles** First make a template by cutting an 11¼in (28.5cm) square in paper, cut the paper square in half diagonally to form a triangle, this is the template shape. Transfer onto card

**CUTTING LAYOUT FOR WCS YE**

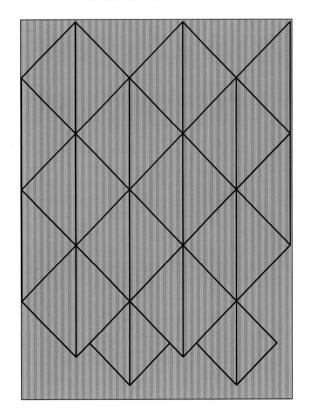

85

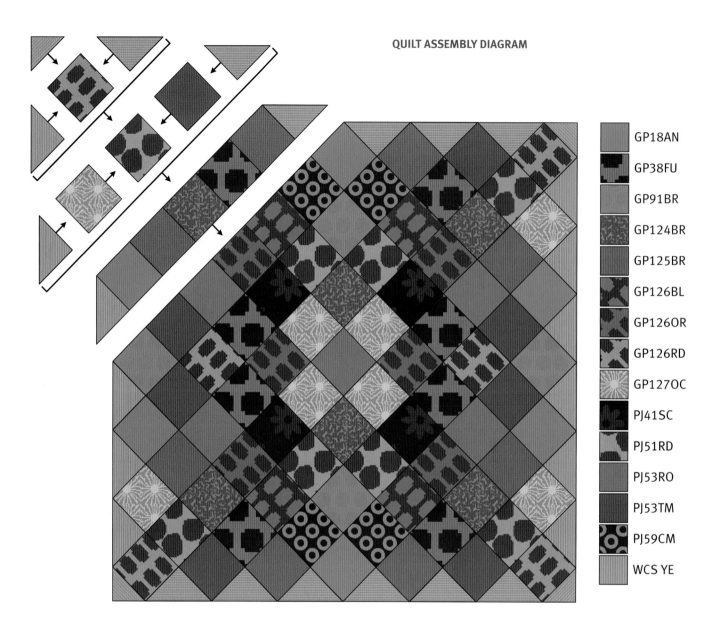

GP18AN
GP38FU
GP91BR
GP124BR
GP125BR
GP126BL
GP126OR
GP126RD
GP127OC
PJ41SC
PJ51RD
PJ53RO
PJ53TM
PJ59CM
WCS YE

or template plastic and cut out. Cut 8in (20.25cm) strips down the length of the fabric as shown in the cutting layout for WCS YE. Align the long side of the triangle template with the stripe direction as shown, this will ensure the long side of the triangle will not have a bias edge. Cut 24 triangles in WCS YE. These triangles are cut oversize and will be trimmed after piecing.

**Corner Setting Triangles** First make a template by cutting an 8½in (21.5cm) square in paper, cut the paper square in half diagonally to form a triangle, this is the template shape. Transfer onto card or template plastic and cut out. Cut 4 triangles as shown in the cutting layout for WCS YE. These triangles are cut oversize and will be trimmed after piecing.

**Binding** Cut 10 strips 2½in (6.5cm) wide across the width of the fabric in GP127BK.

**Backing** Cut 2 pieces 40in x 102in (101.5cm x 259cm), 2 pieces 40in x 23in (101.5 x 58.5cm) and 1 piece 23in x 23in (58.5cm x 58.5cm) in backing fabric.

**MAKING THE QUILT**
Use a ¼in (6mm) seam allowance throughout. Refer to the quilt assembly diagram for fabric placement. Lay out the large squares and setting triangles as shown in the quilt assembly diagram. Carefully separate into diagonal rows and piece the rows. The setting triangles are oversize and will be trimmed once the whole quilt is assembled. Join the rows

to complete the quilt top. Now carefully trim the excess setting triangle fabric making sure to leave a generous ¼in (6mm) OUTSIDE the points of the squares along the quilt edges.

**FINISHING THE QUILT**
Press the quilt top. Seam the backing pieces using a ¼in (6mm) seam allowance to form a piece approx 102in x 102in (259cm x 259cm). Layer the quilt top, batting and backing and baste together (see page 144). Machine quilt in the ditch along all the diagonal seams and then hand quilt a cross in each square using toning perlé embroidery threads. Trim the quilt edges and attach the binding (see page 145).

# geese in flight **

## Roberta Horton

The centre of this quilt is filled with 5 columns of flying geese blocks which are made with 2 triangles (Templates Q and R). The columns are mirrored across the quilt, so that the first and fifth column match as do the second and fourth, the centre column is unique. The columns are interspaced with matching sashing strips. An inner border is added for drama and a simple outer border provides a finishing frame. Roberta describes the design as a 'controlled scrap quilt'.

## SIZE OF QUILT
The finished quilt will measure approx. 78¼in x 87½in (198.75cm x 222.25cm).

## MATERIALS
**Patchwork Fabrics**
SPOT
Duck Egg    GP70DE    ½yd (45cm)
MILLEFIORE
Lilac    GP92LI    ⅝yd (60cm)
PETUNIAS
Blue    PJ50BL    ½yd (45cm)
Green    PJ50GN    ¾yd (70cm)
BRASSICA
Blue    PJ51BL    ¾yd (70cm)
Green    PJ51GN    ⅝yd 60cm)
PICOTTE POPPIES
Pastel    PJ52PT    ⅝yd (60cm)

**Sashing and Border Fabrics**
SPOT
Magenta    GP70MG    ⅝yd (60cm)
BRASSICA
Grey    PJ51GY    2¼yd (2.1m)
PICOTTE POPPIES
Turquoise    PJ52TQ    1⅝yd (1.5m)

**Backing Fabric** 6¼yd (5.7m)
We suggest these fabrics for backing
CABBAGE AND ROSE Blue, GP38BL
PETUNIAS Blue, PJ50BL
BRASSICA Blue, PJ51BL

**Binding**
PAPERWEIGHT
Purple    GP20PU    ¾yd (70cm)

**Batting**
86in x 95in (218.5cm x 241.25cm)

**Quilting thread**
Toning, blue and purple machine quilting threads

Templates

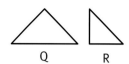

Q       R

## CUTTING OUT
**Template Q** Cut 4¼in (10.75cm) strips across the width of the fabric. Align the template with the long side along the cut edge of the strip, this will ensure the long side of the triangles will not have a bias edge. Each strip will give you 8 triangles per full width. Cut 26 in PJ51GN, 25 in GP92LI, PJ52PT and 24 in GP70DE. Total 100 triangles.
**Template R** Cut 4½in (11.5cm) strips across the width of the fabric, each strip will give you 16 triangles per full width. Cut 4½in (11.5cm) squares, then cut each square diagonally to form 2 triangles using the template as a guide. Handle the triangles carefully as the long edge will be on the bias and stretchy. Cut 80 in PJ50GN, PJ51BL and 40 in PJ50BL. Total 200 triangles.
**Sashing** Down the length of the fabric cut 6 sashing strips 5in x 73in (12.75cm x 185.5cm)
**Inner Border** Cut 8 strips 2in (5cm) wide across the width of the fabric, join as necessary and cut 2 inner borders 2in x 73in (5cm x 185.5cm) for the quilt sides and 2 outer borders 2in x 66¾in (5cm x 169.5cm) for the quilt top and bottom.
**Outer Border** Cut 8 strips 6½in (16.5cm) wide across the width of the fabric, join as necessary and cut 2 outer borders 6½in x 78¾in (16.5cm x 200cm) for the quilt top and bottom and 2 outer borders 6½in x 76in (16.5cm x 193cm) for the quilt sides.

**Binding** Cut 9 strips 2½in (6.5cm) wide across the width of the fabric in GP20PU.

**Backing** Cut 2 pieces 40in x 95in (101.5cm x 241.25cm), 2 pieces 40in x 7in (101.5cm x 17.75cm) and 1 piece 16in x 7in (40.5cm x 17.75cm) in backing fabric.

## MAKING THE BLOCKS
Use a ¼in (6mm) seam allowance throughout. Refer to the quilt assembly diagram for fabric placement. Piece a total of 100 flying geese blocks as shown in block assembly diagram a, the finished block can be seen in diagram b.

## MAKING THE QUILT
Join the flying geese blocks into 5 columns. Note that columns 1 and 5 are identical as are columns 2 and 4. Lay the columns out with the sashing strips and join as shown in the quilt assembly diagram to complete the quilt centre. Add the inner border, sides then top and bottom and finally the outer borders in the same way as shown in the quilt assembly diagram to complete the quilt.

### BLOCK ASSEMBLY DIAGRAMS

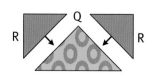
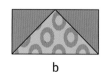

a             b

## QUILT ASSEMBLY DIAGRAM

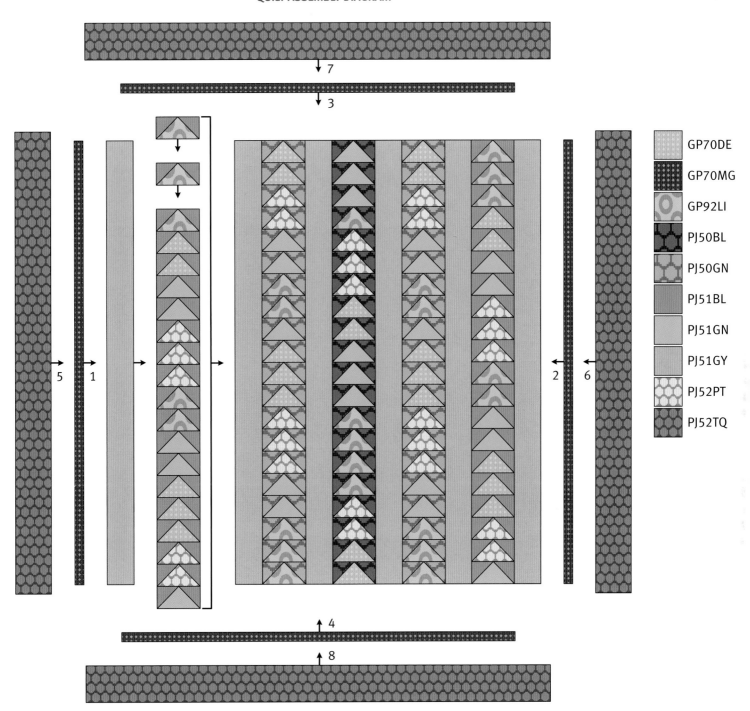

**FINISHING THE QUILT**

Press the quilt top. Seam the backing pieces using a ¼in (6mm) seam allowance to form a piece approx. 86in x 95in (218.5cm x 241.25cm). Layer the quilt top, batting and backing and baste together (see page 144). Using toning quilting thread stitch in the ditch along all the vertical column seams and on both sides of the inner borders. Using blue thread quilt ¼in (6mm) inside the template Q triangles. Quilt 2 serpentine lines down each of the sashing strips using purple thread and finally using blue thread quilt the border with 2 parallel lines offset from the seam by 2in and 4in (5cm and 10.25cm). Trim the quilt edges and attach the binding (see page 145).

# lorna doone **

## Corienne Kramer

The main blocks in this delightful quilt are fussy cut framed squares which finish to 10½in (26.5cm), made using 1 square (Large Square) which is cut to size and 2 rectangles (Short and Long Rectangle), also cut to size. The main blocks are set on point and separated by pieced sashing. The sashing is made up of 1 square (Template BBB) and hourglass blocks pieced using 1 triangle (Template CCC) which are cut in 2 ways depending on their position within the quilt, so please read the cutting instructions carefully. A second triangle (Template N) is used to fill in around the quilt centre edge. The quilt is completed with a simple border with pieced corner posts, made using a third triangle (Template A) which gives the illusion of mitred corners.

## SIZE OF QUILT
The finished quilt will measure approx. 79¼in x 99in (201.25cm x 251.5cm).

## MATERIALS
### Patchwork Fabrics
PAPERWEIGHT
Sludge          GP20SL      ¾yd (70cm)
LOTUS LEAF
Jade            GP29JA      ⅜yd (35cm)
GUINEA FLOWER
Turquoise       GP59TQ      ⅜yd (35cm)
SPOT
Apple           GP70AL      ¾yd (70cm)
Duck Egg        GP70DE      2½yd (2.3m)
ASIAN CIRCLES
Green           GP89GN      ⅜yd (35cm)
Pink            GP89PK      ⅜yd (35cm)
Turquoise       GP89TQ      ⅜yd (35cm)
Yellow          GP89YE      ⅜yd (35cm)
MILLEFIORE
Lilac           GP92LI      ⅜yd (35cm)
BRASSICA
Pastel          PJ51PT      2¼yd (2.1m)

### Border Fabric
SHIRT STRIPES
Midnight Chalk  GP51MC  1¾yd (1.6m)

### Backing Fabric  4¾yd (4.35m)
We suggest these fabrics for backing
GUINEA FLOWER Gold, GP59GD
SHIRT STRIPES, Midnight Chalk, GP51MC

### Binding
SHIRT STRIPES
Cobalt          GP51CB      ⅞yd (80cm)

### Batting
87in x 107in (221cm x 271.75cm)

### Quilting thread
Toning machine quilting thread

## Templates

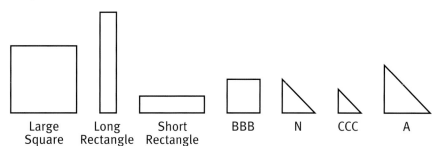

Large Square    Long Rectangle    Short Rectangle    BBB    N    CCC    A

## CUTTING OUT
Please read the cutting instructions carefully as template CCC is cut in 2 ways depending on its position in the quilt, keep the 2 types separate after cutting. Cut the fabric in the order stated to prevent waste.

**Template BBB** Cut 4in (10.25cm) strips across the width of the fabric. Each strip will give you 10 squares per full width. Cut 32 in PJ51PT, 20 in GP29JA, GP59TQ, GP89GN, GP89PK, GP89YE, 16 in GP92LI and 12 in GP89TQ. Total 160 squares.

**Large Square** Fussy cut squares 7½in x 7½in (19cm x 19cm) centring on the cabbage designs. Cut 31 in PJ51PT.

**Template N** Cut a 6¼in (16cm) strip across the width of the fabric in GP70DE, cut 5 squares 6¼in x 6¼in (16cm x 16cm), then cut each square twice diagonally to make 4 triangles using the template as a guide, do not move the patches until both diagonals have been cut. This will ensure the long side of the triangle will not have a bias edge. Total 18 triangles (and 2 spare).

**Long Rectangle** Cut 2¼in (5.75cm) strips across the width of the fabric. Each strip will give you 3 rectangles per full width. Cut 2¼in x 11in (5.75cm x 28cm) rectangles. Cut 62 in GP70DE.

**Short Rectangle** Cut 2¼in (5.75cm) strips across the width of the fabric. Each strip will give you 5 rectangles per full width. Cut 2¼in x 7½in (5.75cm x 19cm) rectangles. Cut 62 in GP70DE.

**Template CCC** For hourglass blocks cut 4¾in (12cm) strips across the width of the fabric. Each strip will give you 32 triangles per full width. Cut squares 4¾in x 4¾in (12cm x 12cm), then cut each square twice diagonally to make 4 triangles using the template as a guide, do not move the patches until both diagonals have been cut. This will ensure the long side of the triangle will not have a bias edge. Cut 96 in GP20SL and GP70AL. Total 192 triangles.

**Template CCC** For quilt centre edges and corners cut 3⅜in (8.5cm) strips across the width of the fabric. Each strip will give you 22 triangles per full width. Cut squares 3⅜in x 3⅜in (8.5cm x 8.5cm), then cut each square once diagonally to make 2 triangles using the template as a guide. This will ensure the short side of the triangle will not have a bias edge when positioned along the quilt centre edges. Cut 32 in GP20SL and 28 in GP70AL. Total 60 triangles.

**Template A** Cut a 5⅞in (15cm) strip across the width of the fabric in GP51MC, cut 4 squares 5⅞in x 5⅞in (15cm x 15cm), align the stripes in the fabric design vertically then cut 2 squares diagonally from top left to bottom right, then cut the other 2 squares diagonally from top right to bottom left. This will enable you to piece 4 half square triangle corner posts with the stripe directions matching the borders to create the illusion of mitred corners.

**Borders** Down the length of the fabric cut 7 strips 5½in (14cm) wide. Join the strips as necessary and cut 2 borders 5½in x 89½in (14cm x 277.25cm) for the quilt sides and 2 borders 5½in x 69¾in (14cm x 177.25cm) in GP51MC for the quilt top and bottom.

**Binding** Cut 10 strips 2½in (6.5cm) wide across the width of the fabric in GP51CB.

**Backing** Cut 2 pieces 40in x 107in (101.5cm x 271.75cm), 2 pieces 40in x 8in (101.5cm x 20.25cm) and 1 piece 28in x 8in (71cm x 20.25cm) in backing fabric.

### MAKING THE BLOCKS

Use a ¼in (6mm) seam allowance throughout. Refer to the quilt assembly diagram for fabric placement. To make a framed square block take a fussy cut large square and join a short rectangles to opposite sides, press, then add a long rectangle to the other 2 sides as shown in block assembly diagram a. The finished block is shown in diagram b. Make 31 framed square blocks.

Using the template CCC triangles cut for hourglass blocks (96 triangles in GP20SL and GP70AL), make 48 hourglass blocks

as shown in block assembly diagrams c and d. The finished hourglass block is shown in diagram e.

Now take the template CCC triangles cut for quilt centre edges and corners, reserve 4 triangles in GP20SL for the corners of the quilt centre. Take the remaining triangles (28 triangles in GP20SL and GP70AL) and make 28 half hourglass blocks, 14 as shown in block assembly diagram f and 14 as shown in diagram g.

Finally make 4 border corner posts, take 2 triangles and align the stripe direction so that they will produce the illusion of a mitred corner, stitch into a half square triangle block, make 4 and reserve until you are ready to add the border to the quilt centre.

### MAKING THE QUILT

Lay out the framed square blocks with the sashing elements, template BBB squares and hourglass blocks as shown in the quilt assembly diagram. You will notice that the framed squares along the edges need trimming to fit, don't do this until the quilt centre is assembled. Fill in along the quilt edges with the template N triangles, the half hourglass blocks, BBB

squares and complete the corners with the 4 reserved template CCC triangles. Separate into diagonal rows, some sashing pieces need to be sub-pieced before the full rows can be assembled, stitch the elements together to form rows as shown in the quilt assembly diagram. Join the rows to complete the quilt centre. Trim the framed squares to fit making sure you leave a ¼in (6mm) seam allowance OUTSIDE the points of the centre squares.

Add the side borders to the quilt centre, then add a pieced corner post to each end of the top and bottom borders, making sure the stripe direction is consistent. Join the top and bottom borders to the centre to complete the quilt.

### FINISHING THE QUILT

Press the quilt top. Seam the backing pieces using a ¼in (6mm) seam allowance to form a piece approx. 87in x 107in (221cm x 271.75cm). Layer the quilt top, batting and backing and baste together (see page 144). Using toning machine quilting thread stitch in the ditch around each framed square. Free motion quilt in the large squares following the cabbage designs in the fabric. In the GP70DE frames free motion quilt a double meander to create a ribbon like effect around each frame and quilt a wide meander along the sashings. In the border free motion quilt in a geometric style following the strip sections of stripes in the fabric design. Trim the quilt edges and attach the binding (see page 145).

**BLOCK ASSEMBLY DIAGRAMS**

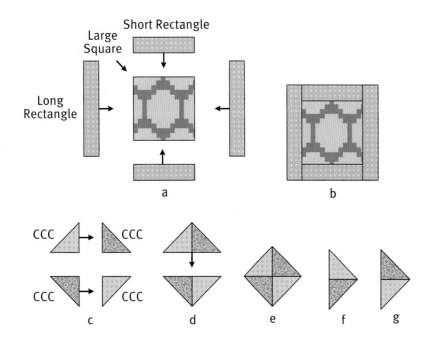

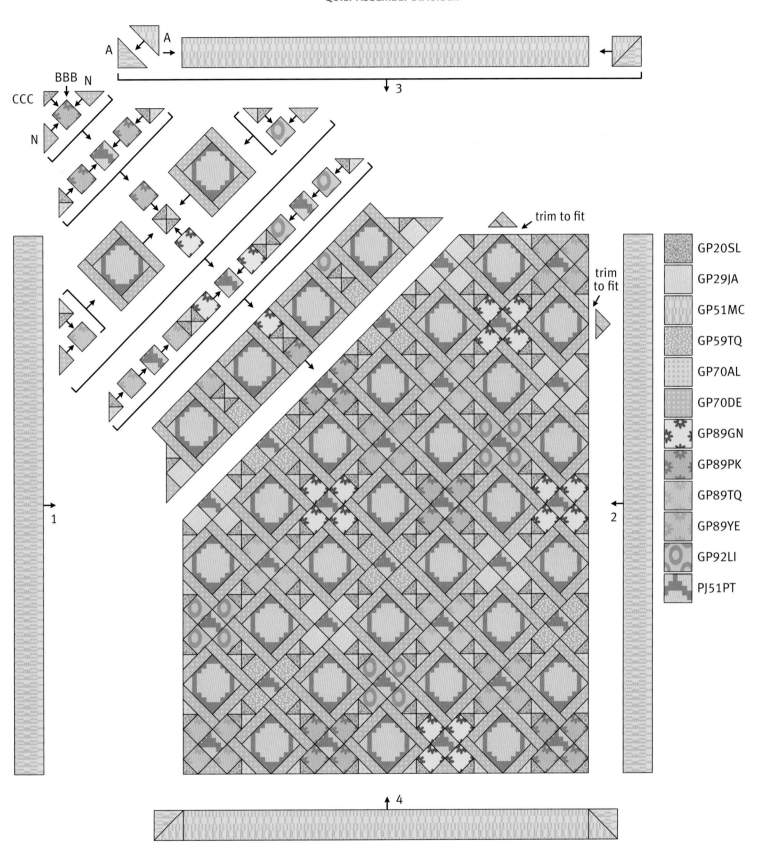

trim to fit

trim to fit

1

2

3

4

A

A

BBB

CCC

N

N

GP20SL
GP29JA
GP51MC
GP59TQ
GP70AL
GP70DE
GP89GN
GP89PK
GP89TQ
GP89YE
GP92LI
PJ51PT

# dreamy hexagons **

## Liza Prior Lucy

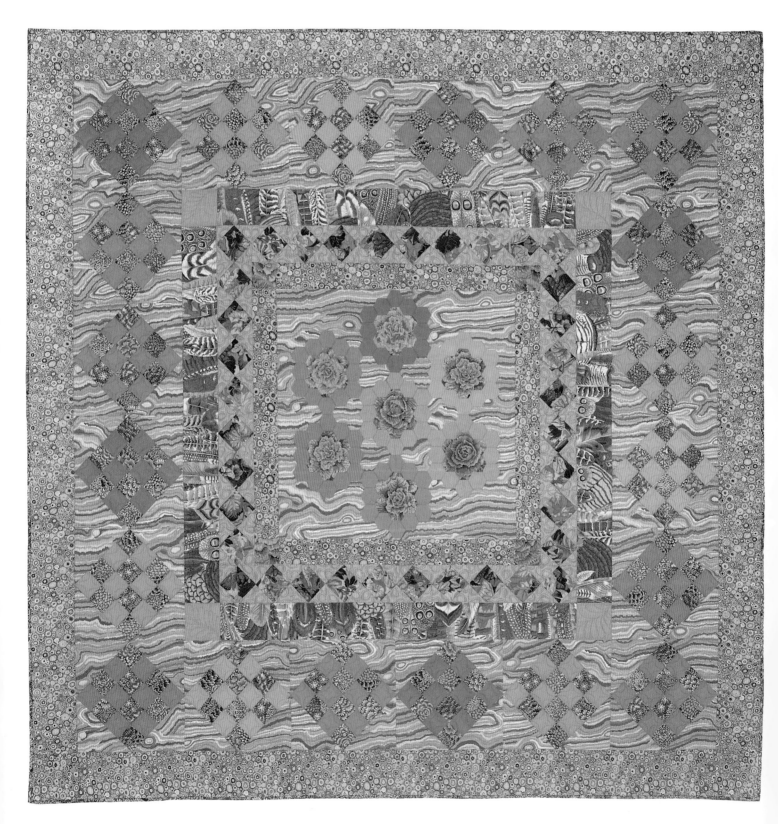

This delightful medallion style quilt is built in a series of layers around a centre panel. The centre has English paper pieced hexagons (Template JJ) which are joined into rings and appliquéd over fussy cut squares of fabric to fill the middles of the rings. The rings are then joined and appliquéd to a background panel. Border 1 is simple with square corner posts (Template KK), Border 2 is pieced of 'square in a square' blocks using a square (Template LL) and a triangle (Template MM). Border 3 is simple, again with square corner posts (Template B), Border 4 is pieced, checkerboard blocks are made using a square (Template NN) then set on point using a triangle (Template OO). The final border (Border 5) is simple this time without corner posts.

## SIZE OF QUILT

The finished quilt will measure approx. 82in x 82in (208.25cm x 208.25cm)

## MATERIALS

**Patchwork and Border Fabrics**
PAPERWEIGHT
Sludge   GP20SL   1¾ yd (1.6m)
ABORIGINAL DOTS
Silver   GP70SV   ⅝yd (60cm)
ORIENTAL TREES
Stone   GP129ST   ⅞yd (70cm)
JUPITER
Stone   GP131ST   2⅝yd (2.4m)
GRANDIOSE
Grey   PJ13GY   ½yd (45cm)
BRASSICA
Grey   PJ51GY   1yd (90cm)
FEATHERS
Grey   PJ55GY   ⅝yd (60cm)
SHOT COTTON
Aqua   SC77   ⅜yd (35cm)
Dill   SC100DL   ⅜yd (35cm)
Latte   SC100LA   ¼yd (25cm)
Pumpkin   SC100PN   ⅜yd (35cm)
Quartz   SC100QZ   ⅜yd (35cm)
Squash   SC100SQ   ⅜yd (35cm)
Violet   SC100VI   ⅜yd (35cm)

**Backing Fabric** 6¼yd (5.75m)
We suggest these fabrics for backing
BRASSICA Grey, PJ51GY
GRANDIOSE Grey PJ13GY
ORIENTAL TREES Stone, GP129ST

## Templates

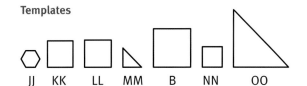

JJ   KK   LL   MM   B   NN   OO

**Binding**
ORIENTAL TREES
Stone   GP129ST   ¾yd (70cm)

**Batting**
90in x 90in (228.5cm x 228.5cm)

**Quilting thread**
Toning machine quilting thread

**You will also need**
84 hexagon papers 1in (2.5cm) finished side. These can be purchased or cut from standard copier paper using the template provided.

## CUTTING OUT

Please read the cutting instructions carefully as some pieces are fussy cut.
**Centre Panel**
**Centre Panel** Cut a 28in x 28in (71cm x 71cm) square in GP131ST. This panel is oversized and will be trimmed later.
**Template JJ** Cut 84 papers using the paper template. Using the fabric template (JJ) cut 12 in SC77, SC100DL, SC100LA, SC100PN, SC100QZ, SC100SQ and SC100VI. Total 84 hexagons.
**Background Squares** Fussy cut 7 squares 6in x 6in (15.25cm x 15.25cm) centring on the cabbage designs in PJ51GY.
**Border 1**
Cut 4 borders 3¼in x 27in (8.25cm x 68.5cm) in GP20SL.
**Template KK** Cut 4 squares 3¼in x 3¼in (8.25cm x 8.25cm) in PJ51GY.
**Border 2**
**Template LL** Cut 3⅜in (8.5cm) strips across the width of the fabric, each strip will give you 11 squares per full width. Cut 36 in PJ13GY.
**Template MM** Cut 2⅞in (7.25cm) strips across the width of the fabric, each strip will give you 26 triangles per full width. Cut 144 in GP71SV.
**Border 3**
Cut 4 borders 4½in x 40½in (11.5cm x 103cm) in PJ55GY.
**Template B** Cut 4 squares 4½in x 4½in (11.5cm x 11.5cm) in SC100LA.

## Border 4

**Template NN** Cut 2⅝in (6.75cm) strips across the width of the fabric, each strip will give you 15 squares per full width. Cut 160 in GP129ST, 32 in SC77, SC100VI, 24 in SC100DL, SC100PN, SC100QZ and SC100SQ. Total 320 squares.
**Template OO** Cut 6⅞in (17.5cm) strips across the width of the fabric, each strip will give you 10 triangles per full width. Cut 40 squares 6⅞in x 6⅞in (17.5cm x 17.5cm) in GP131ST. Line up all the squares with the lines in the fabric design running horizontally. Using the template as a guide fussy cut 20 squares diagonally from top left to bottom right to form 40 triangles, then fussy cut the other 20 squares diagonally from top right to bottom left to form 40 triangles. Total 80 triangles.
**Border 5**
Cut 8 strips 5½in (14cm) wide across the width of the fabric, join as necessary and cut 2 borders 5½in x 82½ (14cm x 209.5cm) in for the quilt top and bottom and 2 borders 5½in x 72½ (14cm x 184.25cm) in for the quilt sides in GP20SL.

**Binding** Cut 9 strips 2½in (6.5cm) wide across the width of the fabric in GP129ST.

**Backing** Cut 2 pieces 40in x 90in (101.5cm x 228.5cm), 2 pieces 40in x 11in (101.5 x 28cm) and 1 piece 11in x 11in (28cm x 28cm) in backing fabric.

## MAKING CENTRE PANEL

Use a ¼in (6mm) seam allowance throughout. Refer to the quilt assembly diagram for fabric placement. Take a hexagon paper and place it centrally to the wrong side of a template JJ fabric hexagon, use a tiny dot of washable glue stick or a pin to hold the paper and fabric together as shown in diagram a. Fold the fabric tightly over the first side of the paper hexagon, finger press and baste into place using large stitches as shown in diagram b, continue folding and basting until

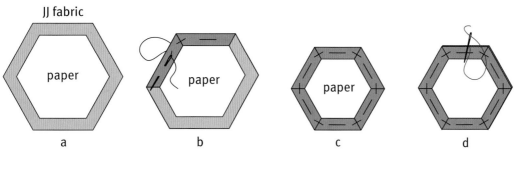

JJ fabric

a     b     c     d

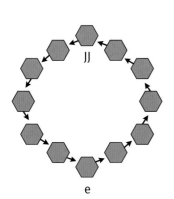

e

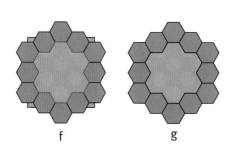

f     g

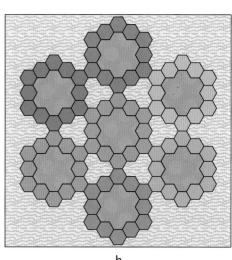

h

the hexagon is complete, see diagram c. Baste all the hexagons to papers, 12 in each of the Shot Cotton colours. Take 2 hexagons and place right sides together matching the edges carefully. Starting with a knotted thread slip your needle between the paper and the fabric and come out right on the corner of the hexagon. Whip stitch through the very edge of the fabrics along one side as shown in diagram d, finish with a double stitch to secure. Add the next hexagon as shown in diagram e and continue until the ring is complete.

It is optional whether you do the appliqué with the hexagon papers still basted to the fabric. It is easier to take the papers out first, but you must handle the hexagons very gently. To do this heavily starch and press the rings on the back and front with the papers still in, then carefully remove the papers. Baste the seams allowances into place around the inner and outer edge of the rings to keep the shape perfect.

Lay the completed ring over a square of PJ51GY fabric as shown in diagram f pin thoroughly and slip stitch into place around the inner ring. Trim the excess PJ51GY fabric back to leave a ¼in (6mm) allowance. A completed ring can be seen in diagram g. Make 7 rings.

Join the 7 rings using the whip stitch technique. The layout is shown in diagram h, there should be 6 gaps around the centre ring. Lay the joined rings centrally over the centre panel of GP131ST (the lines in the fabric design should run horizontally, see the photograph). Pin thoroughly and slip stitch the rings to the background around the outer edge and around the gaps. Trim the excess GP131ST fabric from behind the rings to leave a ¼in (6mm) allowance. Trim the centre panel equally to 27in (68.5cm) square. If you left the hexagon papers in you can now remove them.

## ADDING THE BORDERS

### Border 1

Add a border to each side of the centre panel, join a corner post to each end of the remaining 2 borders and add these to the top and bottom of the centre panel as shown in the quilt centre assembly diagram.

### Border 2

Piece 36 'square in a square' blocks as shown in block assembly diagrams i and j. The finished block is shown in diagram k. Join blocks into 2 strips of 8 and add to the quilt sides. Join the remaining blocks into 2 strips of 10 and add to the quilt top and bottom as shown in the quilt centre assembly diagram.

### Border 3

Add a border to each side of the quilt, join a corner post to each end of the remaining 2 borders and add these to the top and bottom of the quilt as shown in the quilt assembly diagram.

### Border 4

Piece 20 checkerboard blocks as shown in block assembly diagram l.

## QUILT CENTRE ASSEMBLY DIAGRAM

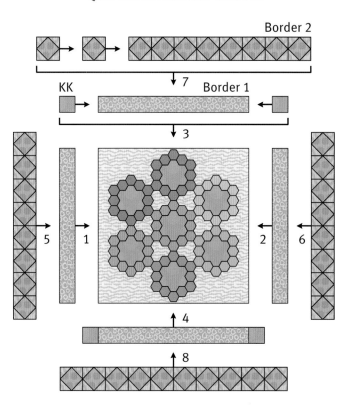

## BLOCK ASSEMBLY DIAGRAMS

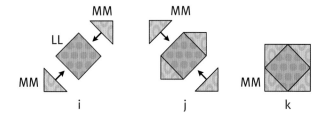

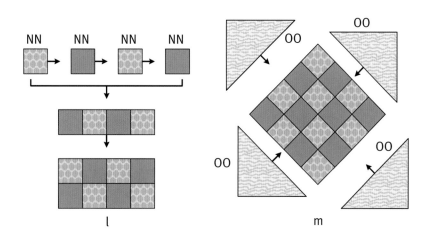

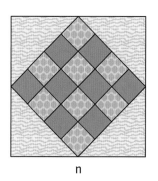

**QUILT ASSEMBLY DIAGRAM**

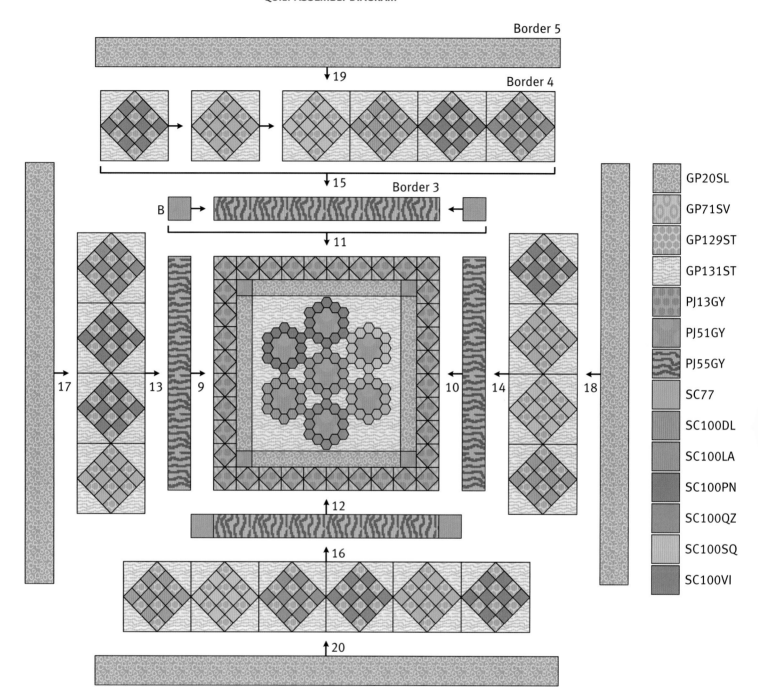

Add setting triangles to each block as shown in diagram m. Ensure the lines in the GP131ST Jupiter fabric all run horizontally, check the photograph for help with this. The finished block is shown in diagram n. Join blocks into 2 strips of 4 and add to the quilt sides. Join the remaining blocks into 2 strips of 6 and add to the quilt top and bottom as shown in the quilt assembly diagram.

**Border 5**
Add the shorter side borders to the quilt centre followed by the longer top and bottom borders to complete the quilt.

**FINISHING THE QUILT**
Press the quilt top. Seam the backing pieces using a ¼in (6mm) seam allowance to form a piece approx. 90in x 90in (228.5cm x 228.5cm). Layer the

quilt top, batting and backing and baste together (see page 144). Using toning machine quilting thread quilt in the ditch in the main seams, then meander quilt following the fabric designs in the centre panel and borders 2, 3 and 4. Trim the quilt edges and attach the binding (see page 145).

# diagonal bricks *

Judy Baldwin

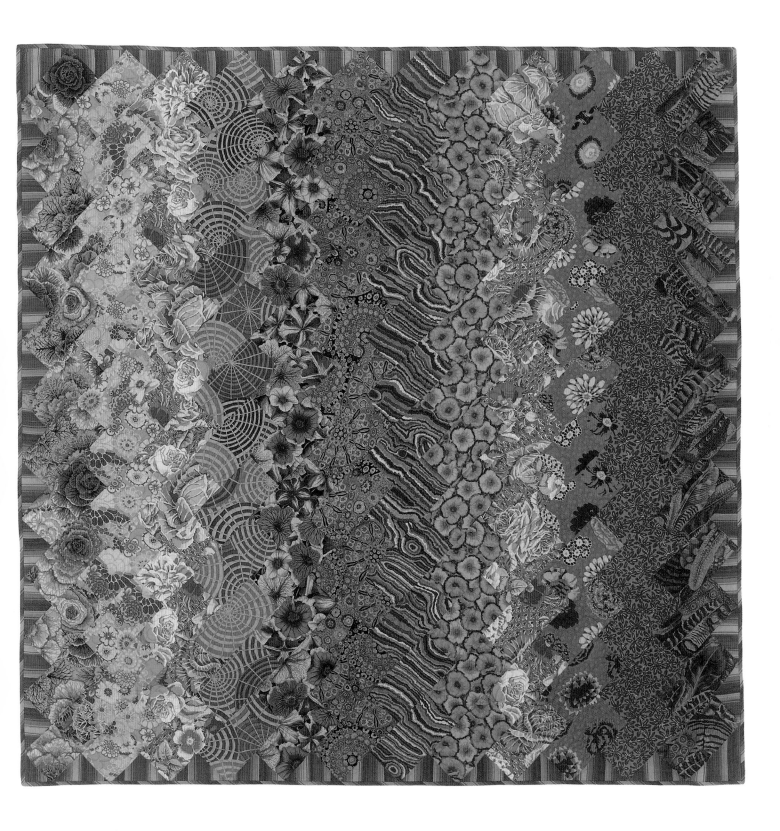

This quilt is made using rectangles (Template SS) which are pieced into diagonal rows. The fabrics are placed in sequence so that they line up in vertical columns when the quilt is complete. The row ends are completed with triangles (Template VV), with 2 further triangles (Templates TT and UU) used to complete the quilt corners.

### SIZE OF QUILT

The finished quilt will measure approx. 70¾in x 70¾in (179.75cm x 179.75cm).

### MATERIALS

**Patchwork Fabrics**

| DAISY CHAIN | | | |
| --- | --- | --- | --- |
| Ochre | BM34OC | ½yd (45cm) | |

CABBAGE AND ROSE
Wood        GP38WD      ⅞yd (80cm)
ASIAN CIRCLES
Orange      GP89OR      ½yd (45cm)
BIG BLOOMS
Brown       GP91BR      ½yd (45cm)
MILLEFIORE
Brown       GP92BR      ½yd (45cm)
PARASOLS
Ochre       GP127OC     ½yd (45cm)
JUPITER
Brown       GP131BR     ⅝yd (60cm)
PETUNIAS
Ochre       PJ50OC      ½yd (45cm)
BRASSICA
Brown       PJ51BR      ½yd (45cm)
PICOTTE POPPIES
Ochre       PJ52OC      ½yd (45cm)
FEATHERS
Brown       PJ55BR      ⅝yd (60cm)
WOVEN EXOTIC STRIPE
Dusk        WES DU      ¾yd (70cm)

**Backing Fabric** 4¾yd (4.35m)
We suggest these fabrics for backing
CACTUS DAHLIAS Gold, PJ54GD
CABBAGE AND ROSE Wood, GP38WD
BRASSICA Brown, PJ51BR

**Binding**
WOVEN EXOTIC STRIPE
Dusk        WES DU      ¾yd (70cm)

**Batting**
79in x 79in (200.5cm x 200.5cm)

**Quilting thread**
Toning machine quilting thread

**Templates**

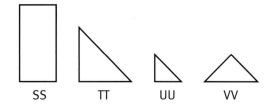

SS          TT          UU          VV

### CUTTING OUT

**Template SS** For fabrics GP131BR and PJ55BR Cut 8½in (21.5cm) strips across the width of the fabric, Each strip will give you 8 rectangles per full width. Cut 8½in x 4½in (21.5cm x 11.5cm) rectangles, Cut 12 in GP131BR and PJ55BR. For the other print fabrics cut 4½in (11.5cm) strips across the width of the fabric. Each strip will give you 4 rectangles per full width. Cut 8½in x 4½in (21.5cm x 11.5cm) rectangles, cut 24 in GP38WD, 12 in BM34OC, GP89OR, GP91BR, GP92BR, GP127OC, PJ50OC, PJ51BR and PJ52OC. Total 144 rectangles.

**Template VV** Cut 3½in (9cm) strips across the width of the fabric, Each strip will give you 10 triangles per full width.

Align the long side of the triangle with the cut edge of the strip, this will ensure the long side of the triangle will not have a bias edge and the stripes will run correctly. Cut 44 in WES DU.

**Template TT** Cut a square 6½in x 6½in (16.5cm x 16.5cm) in WES DU. With the stripes vertical cut the square diagonally from the top right to the bottom left to form 2 triangles. This will ensure the stripes will run correctly.

**Template UU** Cut a square 3¾in x 3¾in (9.5 cm x 9.5cm) in WES DU. With the stripes vertical cut the square diagonally from the top left to the bottom right to form 2 triangles. This will ensure the stripes will run correctly.

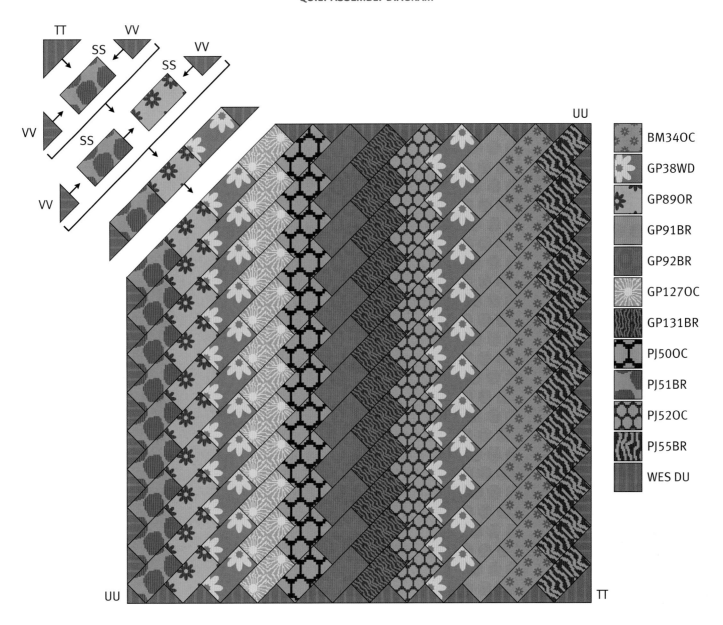

**Binding** Cut 8⅛yd (7.4m) of 2½in (6.5cm) wide bias binding in WES DU.

**Backing** Cut 2 pieces 40in x 79in (101.5cm x 200.5cm) in backing fabric.

**MAKING THE QUILT**
Use a ¼in (6mm) seam allowance throughout. Refer to the quilt assembly diagram for fabric placement. Take the GP38WD template SS rectangles and separate into light and dark so you

have 2 sets of 12, use the lights on the left side of the quilt and the darks on the right side. Lay out the template SS rectangles in sequence as shown in the quilt assembly diagram, separate into diagonal rows and use the template VV triangles to complete the row ends. Use the template TT and UU triangles in the corners of the quilt. Join the rectangles and triangles into rows, then join the rows to complete the quilt.

**FINISHING THE QUILT**
Press the quilt top. Seam the backing pieces using a ¼in (6mm) seam allowance to form a piece approx. 79in x 79in (200.5cm x 200.5cm). Layer the quilt top, batting and backing and baste together (see page 144). Using toning machine quilting thread free motion quilt in an all over floral design following motifs in the fabric designs if you wish. Trim the quilt edges and attach the binding (see page 145).

# cartwheel **

Liza Prior Lucy

For this striking quilt brightly coloured foundation pieced fans are appliquéd to opposite corners of background squares (cut to size) and arranged to form mismatched 'wheels' at the intersections. Each foundation fan is made up of 6 'spokes' which alternate dark and light. The curved edge of each fan is embellished with a piece of rick rack. The 'wheels' have appliquéd centres which also spill onto the border. The background squares are straight set into rows and surrounded by a border with corner posts (cut to size) to complete the quilt.

## SIZE OF QUILT

The finished quilt will measure approx. 62in x 79in (157.5cm x 200.5cm).

## MATERIALS

### Background and Border Fabrics
PARASOLS

| | | |
|---|---|---|
| Black | GP127BK | 4¾yd (4.4m) |

WOVEN EXOTIC STRIPE

| | | |
|---|---|---|
| Dark | WES DK | 1⅜yd (1.25m) |

### Foundation 'Spoke' Fabrics
Buy 3/8yd (35cm) of each

| | | |
|---|---|---|
| SPOT | Brown | GP70BR |
| SPOT | Fuchsia | GP70FU |
| SPOT | Green | GP70GN |
| SPOT | Magenta | GP70MG |
| SPOT | Orange | GP70OR |
| SPOT | Pond | GP70PO |
| SPOT | Purple | GP70PU |
| SPOT | Sapphire | GP70SP |
| SPOT | Tobacco | GP70TO |
| ABORIGINAL DOTS | Cantaloupe | GP71CA |
| ABORIGINAL DOTS | Charcoal | GP71CC |
| ABORIGINAL DOTS | Gold | GP71GD |
| ABORIGINAL DOTS | Ocean | GP71ON |
| ABORIGINAL DOTS | Ochre | GP71OC |
| ABORIGINAL DOTS | Periwinkle | GP71PE |
| ABORIGINAL DOTS | Plum | GP71PL |
| ABORIGINAL DOTS | Pumpkin | GP71PN |
| ABORIGINAL DOTS | Purple | GP71PU |
| ABORIGINAL DOTS | Terracotta | GP71TC |
| OMBRE | Green | GP117GN |
| OMBRE | Pink | GP117PK |
| OMBRE | Red | GP117RD |

Backing Fabric 5⅜yd (4.7m)
We suggest these fabrics for backing
MILLEFIORE Red, GP92RD
BEGONIA LEAVES Magenta, PJ18MG

### Binding
ABORIGINAL DOTS

| | | |
|---|---|---|
| Periwinkle | GP71PE | ¾yd (70cm) |

### Batting
70in x 87in (177.75cm x 221cm)

### Quilting thread
Medium neutral machine quilting thread

### You will also need
An assortment of medium and jumbo rick rack in bright colours total 23yd (21m)

### Templates
This quilt uses the foundation pattern and circle templates printed on page 141.

### CUTTING OUT
**Background Squares** Cut 9in (22.75cm) strips across the width of the fabric. Each strip will give you 4 squares per full width. Cut 48 squares 9in x 9in (22.75cm x 22.75cm) in GP127BK.
**Corner Posts** Fussy cut 4 squares 6in x 6in (15.25cm x 15.25cm) centring on a spiral in the fabric design in GP127BK.
**Appliqué Centres** Make a transparent plastic template using the template provided and fussy cut 2½in (6.25cm) circles centring on the centre of the spirals. Check the photograph for help with this. Cut 32 in GP127BK.
**Borders** Cut 7 strips 6in (15.25cm) wide across the width of the fabric in WES DK. Join the strips end to end matching the stripe pattern and cut 2 borders 6in x 68½in (15.25cm x 174cm) for the quilt sides and 2 borders 6in x 51½in (15.25cm x 130.75cm) for the quilt top and bottom.
**Foundation 'Spokes'** For each fan you will need 6 'spokes', 3 dark and 3 light. For fan sizes A, B and C cut rectangles 4⅞in x 1¾in (12.5cm x 4.5cm). You will need a total of 150 light and 150 dark rectangles.
For fan sizes D, E and F cut rectangles 8in x 2½in (20.25cm x 6.25cm). You will need a total of 138 light and 138 dark rectangles.

**Binding** Cut 8 strips 2½in (6.5cm) wide across the width of the fabric in GP71PE.

**Backing** Cut 2 pieces 40in x 87in (101.5cm x 221cm) in backing fabric.

### FOUNDATION PIECING

The instructions show a type F fan. For the diagrams RS = Right side, WS = Wrong Side. The foundation papers have a number in each section, this is the order in which pieces are added. Trace or photocopy 96 copies of the foundation pattern on page 141 (you may wish to make extra copies for practice), low quality photocopy paper works well as it tears easily. The same pattern is used for all the sizes, but trimmed on the curved lines. Cut out the foundation fans so that you have a ¼in (6mm) seam allowance on the 2 straight sides as shown on the pattern. The curve is cut WITHOUT a seam allowance, BUT you must leave enough fabric along the curved edge to cut a ¼in (6mm) seam allowance when the foundation piecing is complete. Cut 14 A foundation papers, 18 B papers, 18 C papers, 18 D papers, 18 E papers and 10 F papers.

### Stage 1

The exact placement of the spoke fabrics is not important, just the general light/dark placement. Select 3 light and 3 dark 'spoke' rectangles. Always start with a dark fabric for position 1. Take a dark rectangle and a light rectangle place them right sides together. Turn the foundation paper face down and place fabric over section 1 of the paper with the dark fabric next to the paper as shown in the foundation piecing stage 1 diagram.

### Stage 2

Holding the paper and fabric in place turn the paper over so that the sewing lines are visible. To check the fabric positioning use 2 or 3 pins to secure the fabric along the sewing line ensuring that the fabric edges extend ¼in (6mm) beyond the line between sections 1 and 2. Flip the fabric open to check both section 1 and section 2 will be completely covered by fabric, including all the seam allowance (also make sure there will be enough fabric extending beyond the curve to cut a ¼in (6mm) allowance when piecing

is complete). Holding the paper up to the light is a good way to check. Adjust the fabric positions if necessary, then pin in place ready for stitching. Set your machine to a short stitch, this will perforate the paper and make removal easier later. With the paper upmost stitch on the line between sections 1 and 2, as shown in the stage 2 diagram.

### Stage 3

Turn the paper over and open out the 2 fabric rectangles, press without using steam as it can wrinkle the paper.

### Stage 4

Fold the foundation paper on the next sewing line, in this case between sections 2 and 3, as shown in the stage 4 diagram.

### Stage 5

Trim the fabric to ¼in (6mm) beyond the paper, as shown in the stage 5 diagram.

### Stage 6

Take the next rectangle, dark in this case, and match to the trimmed edge of the previous fabric, pin along the sewing line and flip it back and check it will cover section 3 and seam allowances once stitched. Stitch on the sewing line between sections 2 and 3, as shown in the stage 6 diagram.

In the same manner as stages 3–6 open out the fabric, press, fold the paper on the next sewing line and trim to ¼in (6mm) beyond the next sewing line. Add the next rectangle. Keep doing this until all the sections are covered. Trim away any excess fabric along the straight edges of the paper and trim the curved edge leaving a ¼in (6mm) seam allowance BEYOND the paper. There are many seams meeting at the middle of the fan making it quite lumpy, this will be cut away later so do not be concerned. Take the fan and fold the curved seam allowance over the paper arc (be careful not to fold the paper) and press well with starch. Remove the foundation paper. Make 96 fans in the sizes detailed earlier.

### MAKING THE BLOCKS

Use a ¼in (6mm) seam allowance throughout. Refer to the quilt assembly

### BLOCK ASSEMBLY DIAGRAM

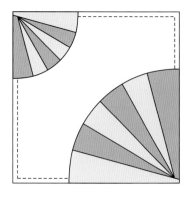

diagram for fan positioning. Prepare 32 appliqué centres using the card template method described in the Patchwork Knowhow section in the back of the book. Take 2 fans and place over opposite corners of a background square matching the raw straight edges carefully as shown in the block assembly diagram, pin into place. Using a neutral thread top stitch along the curve about 1/16in (2mm) from the edge. Next top stitch a piece of rick rack along the curve using a matching thread just below the first top stitching line. Trim the background fabric away from behind the fans leaving a ¼in (6mm) seam allowance. Press carefully. Make 48 blocks.

### MAKING THE QUILT

Use a design wall to lay out the blocks. Sew the blocks into 8 rows of 6 blocks. Join the rows together and press well. As shown on the lower section of the quilt assembly diagram appliqué a centre to the middle of each full 'wheel' and carefully cut away the lumpy fan centres from behind leaving a scant ¼in (6mm) seam allowance. Add the side borders to the quilt centre then add a corner post to each end of the top and bottom borders. Join the top and bottom borders to the centre. Appliqué a centre to the middle of each partial 'wheel' along the border edges and carefully cut away the lumpy fan centres from behind leaving a scant ¼in (6mm) seam allowance to complete the quilt.

### FINISHING THE QUILT

Press the quilt top. Seam the backing pieces using a ¼in (6mm) seam allowance to form a piece approx 70in

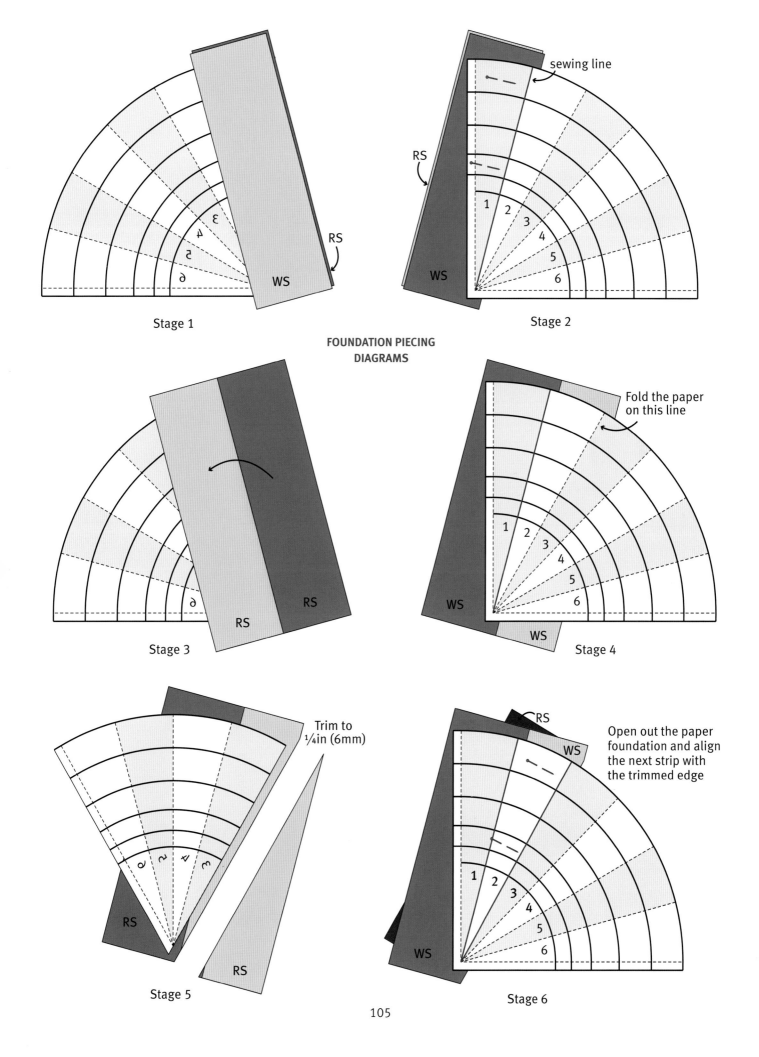

Stage 1

Stage 2

**FOUNDATION PIECING
DIAGRAMS**

sewing line

RS

WS

Stage 3

Fold the paper
on this line

Stage 4

Trim to
¼in (6mm)

Stage 5

RS

WS

Open out the paper
foundation and align
the next strip with
the trimmed edge

Stage 6

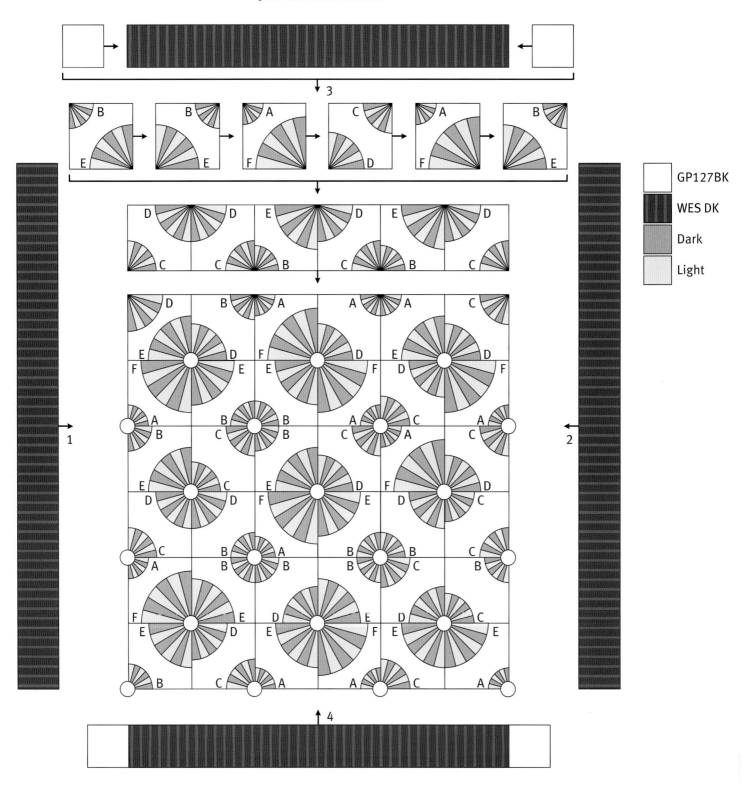

GP127BK

WES DK

Dark

Light

x 87in (177.75cm x 221cm). Layer the quilt top, batting and backing and baste together (see page 144). Using a medium neutral machine quilting thread quilt the background Parasols fabric following the spokes in the fabric design. On the 'wheels' quilt a zig zag pattern in layers around the centres and in the border follow the stripes about every 1 to 2in (2.5cm to 5cm). Trim the quilt edges and attach the binding (see page 145).

# marmalade *

Liza Prior Lucy

107

This quilt is made using traditional Snowball blocks, the shapes are an octagon and four triangles, in this case it is made 'the easy way' by using a large square, cut to size and 4 small squares, again cut to size, for each block. The small squares are placed over the corners of the large squares and stitched diagonally. They are then trimmed and flipped back to replace the corners of the large square. The Snowball blocks are alternated with 25–patch checkerboard blocks pieced using the same small squares.

Both blocks finish at 7½in (19cm). The blocks are set in straight rows and are then surrounded by a pieced border using the same small square. The fabrics used in this quilt are separated into 2 colourways, orange (orange, pink, purple and brown) and aqua (aqua, blue, lime and yellow). The exact positioning of the fabrics is not important, just spread the colours evenly sticking to the overall checkerboard layout.

## SIZE OF QUILT
The finished quilt will measure approx. 88½in x 88½in (224.75cm x 224.75cm).

## MATERIALS
**Patchwork and Border Fabrics**
GRANDIFLORA

| | | |
|---|---|---|
| Tomato | PJ53TM | 3yd (2.75m) |

**Orange Colourway** Buy ½yd (45cm) of each fabric

| | | |
|---|---|---|
| PAPERWEIGHT | Paprika | GP20PP |
| LOTUS LEAF | Wine | GP29WN |
| SPOT | Fuchsia | GP70FU |
| SPOT | Magenta | GP70MG |
| SPOT | Orange | GP70OR |
| SPOT | Royal | GP70RY |
| ABORIGINAL DOTS | Pumpkin | GP71PN |
| ABORIGINAL DOTS | Purple | GP71PU |
| MILLEFIORE | Tomato | GP92TM |
| PLINK | Red | GP109RD |

**Aqua Colourway** Buy ½yd (45cm) of each fabric

| | | |
|---|---|---|
| ROMAN GLASS | Leafy | GP01LF |
| SPOT | Duck Egg | GP70DE |
| SPOT | Pond | GP70PO |
| SPOT | Turquoise | GP70TQ |
| ABORIGINAL DOTS | Delft | GP71DF |
| ABORIGINAL DOTS | Leaf | GP71LF |
| ABORIGINAL DOTS | Ochre | GP71OC |
| ASIAN CIRCLES | Chartreuse | GP89CT |
| MILLEFIORE | Green | GP92GN |
| PLINK | Turquoise | GP109TQ |

**Backing Fabric** 7⅛yd (6.5m)
We suggest these fabrics for backing
MILLEFIORE Tomato, GP92TM
LOTUS LEAF Wine, GP29WN
OMBRE Pink, GP117PK

**Binding**
OMBRE

| | | |
|---|---|---|
| Pink | GP117PK | ⅞yd (80cm) |

**Batting**
96in x 96in (244cm x 244cm)

**Quilting thread**
Toning machine quilting thread

**Templates**

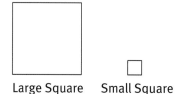

Large Square    Small Square

## CUTTING OUT
**Large Square** Cut 8in (20.25cm) strips across the width of the fabric. Each strip will give you 5 squares per full width. Cut 60 squares 8in x 8in (20.25cm x 20.25cm) in PJ53TM.
**Small Squares** Cut 2in (5cm) strips across the width of the fabric. Each strip will give you 20 squares per full width. Cut 2in (5cm) squares. Cut 1200 in Aqua colourway fabrics and 1021 in Orange colourway fabrics. Total 2221 squares.

**Binding** Cut 10⅛yd (9.25m) of 2½in (6.5cm) wide bias binding in GP117PK.

**Backing** Cut 2 pieces 40in x 96in (101.5cm x 244), 2 pieces 40in x 17in (101.5cm x 43.25cm) and 1 piece 17in x 17in (43.25cm x 43.25cm) in backing fabric.

## MAKING THE BLOCKS
Use a ¼in (6mm) seam allowance throughout. Refer to the quilt assembly diagram for the general colour distribution. The snowball blocks are pieced using 1 large square in PJ53TM and 4 small squares in Aqua colourway.

## BLOCK ASSEMBLY DIAGRAMS

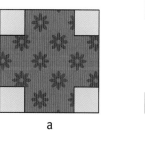

a    b    c

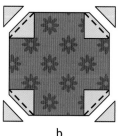

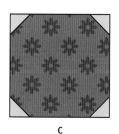

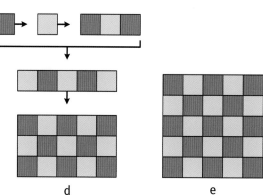

d    e

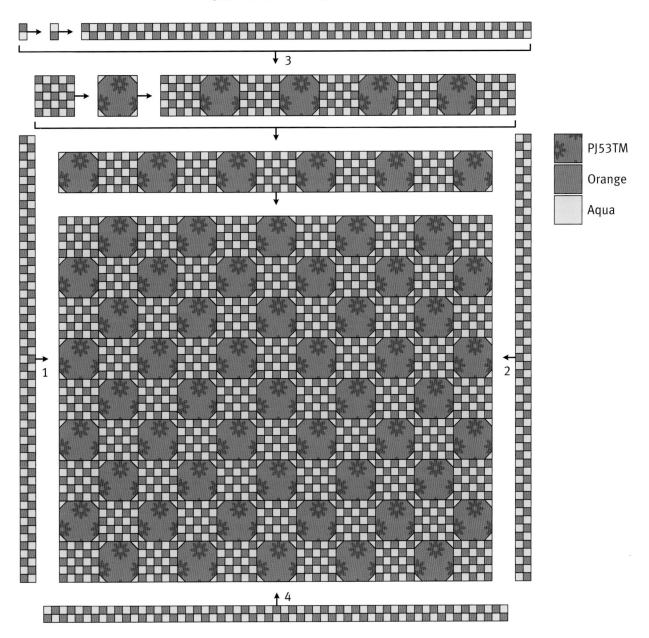

Legend:
- PJ53TM
- Orange
- Aqua

Piece a total of 60 blocks as shown in block assembly diagrams a and b, the finished block is shown in diagram c. Next piece 61 checkerboard blocks as shown in diagram d, each block has 13 Orange colourway and 12 Aqua colourway small squares. Note that every checkerboard block has Orange colourway squares in the outside corners. Always press the seams towards the Orange colourway squares then the seams will nest and make matching easier. The finished block can be seen in diagram e.

**MAKING THE QUILT**

Lay out the snowball blocks and checkerboard blocks alternately as shown in the quilt assembly diagram. Piece the blocks into 11 rows of 11 blocks, join the rows to complete the quilt centre. Join small squares into checkerboard borders. Make sure that the checkerboard pattern will continue into the borders from the quilt centre when piecing the border sections. Piece 2 borders 2 squares by 55 squares for the quilt sides and 2 borders 2 squares x 59 squares for the quilt top and bottom, again pressing towards the Orange colourway squares.

Add the side borders followed by the top and bottom borders to the quilt centre to complete the quilt.

**FINISHING THE QUILT**

Press the quilt top. Seam the backing pieces using a ¼in (6mm) seam allowance to form a piece approx. 96in x 96in (244cm x 244cm). Layer the quilt top, batting and backing and baste together (see page 144). Using toning machine quilting thread stitch in a meander pattern across the whole surface of the quilt. Trim the quilt edges and attach the binding (see page 145).

# paper dolls **

Brandon Mably

110

The delightful 'paper doll' blocks in this quilt are made using a square (Template J), 5 rectangles (Templates H, K, L, O and P), a triangle (Template N) and a lozenge (Template M). The blocks finish to 8½in (21.5cm) square and are set in straight rows. The rows are offset by a half block and the ends of alternate rows are filled with a large rectangle (cut to size). The quilt is finished with a simple border with corner posts.

## SIZE OF QUILT
The finished quilt will measure approx.
50½in x 59in (128.25cm x 150cm).

## MATERIALS
### Patchwork and Border Fabrics
RINGS
| Pink | BM15PK | ¼yd (25cm) |
| Sky | BM15SK | ¼yd (25cm) |

SAND DOLLAR
| Brown | BM31BR | ⅛yd (15cm) |
| Green | BM31GN | ⅛yd (15cm) |
| Orange | BM31OR | ⅛yd (15cm) |
| Yellow | BM31YE | ⅛yd (15cm) |

SAINT CLEMENTS
| Blue | BM32BL | ¼yd (25cm) |
| Magenta | BM32MG | ¼yd (25cm) |

DAISY CHAIN
| Blue | BM34BL | ¼yd (25cm) |
| Yellow | BM34YE | ¼yd (25cm) |

LOTTO
| Magenta | BM35MG | 1½yd (1.4m) |

NETS
| Green | BM36GN | ⅜yd (35cm) |
| Pink | BM36PK | ⅜yd (35cm) |

MAD PLAID
| Autumn | BM37AU | ⅛yd (15cm) |
| Beige | BM37BE | ⅛yd (15cm) |
| Pastel | BM37PT | ⅛yd (15cm) |
| Red | BM37RD | ⅛yd (15cm) |

SPOT
| Lavender | GP70LV | ⅜yd (35cm) |
| Pond | GP70PO | ¼yd (25cm) |

ABORIGINAL DOTS
| Leaf | GP71LF | ¼yd (25cm) |
| Purple | GP71PU | ¼yd (25cm) |

**Backing Fabric** 3⅛yd (2.9m)
We suggest these fabrics for backing
RINGS Sky, BM15SK
SAND DOLLAR Yellow, BM31YE
DAISY CHAIN Blue, BM34BL

**Binding**
SHOT COTTON
| Sunshine | SC35 | ½yd (45cm) |

**Batting**
58in x 67in (147.25cm x 170.25cm)

### Quilting thread
Toning machine quilting thread

### Templates

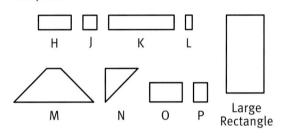

111

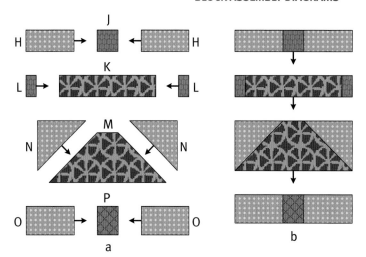

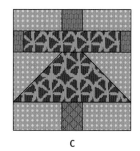

**CUTTING OUT**

Cut the patch shapes in the order specified, always keeping remaining fabric in the largest size possible.
**Template M** Cut 4in (10.25cm) strips across the width of the fabric. Cut 5 in BM15PK, BM15SK, BM32BL, BM32MG, 4 in BM34YE and 3 in BM34BL. Total 27 patches.
**Template K** Cut 7½in x 2in (19cm x 5cm) rectangles. Cut 5 in BM15PK, BM15SK, BM32BL, BM32MG, 4 in BM34YE and 3 in BM34BL. Total 27 rectangles.
**Large Rectangle** Cut 9in x 4¾in (22.75cm x 12cm) rectangles. Cut 3 in BM36GN and BM36PK. Total 6 rectangles.
**Template N** Cut 4⅜in (11cm) squares, then cut each square diagonally to form 2 triangles using the template as a guide. Handle the triangles carefully as the long edge will be on the bias and stretchy. Cut 10 in BM36GN, BM36PK, GP70LV, 8 in GP70PO, GP71LF and GP71PU. Total 54 triangles.
**Template O** Cut 4in x 2½in (10.25cm x 6.25cm) rectangles. Cut 10 in BM36GN, BM36PK, GP70LV, 8 in GP70PO, GP71LF and GP71PU. Total 54 rectangles.
**Template H** Cut 4in x 2in (10.25cm x 5cm) rectangles. Cut 10 in BM36GN, BM36PK, GP70LV, 8 in GP70PO, GP71LF and GP71PU. Total 54 rectangles.
**Template J** Cut 2in x 2in (5cm x 5cm) squares. Cut 7 in BM31BR, BM31OR, BM31YE and 6 in BM31GN. Total 27 squares.

**Template L** Cut 2in x 1¼in (5cm x 3.25cm) rectangles. Cut 14 in BM31BR, BM31OR, BM31YE and 12 in BM31GN. Total 54 rectangles.
**Border Corner Posts** Cut 4½in x 4½in (11.5cm x 11.5cm) squares. Cut 4 in BM37RD.
**Template P** Cut 2½in x 2in (6.25cm x 5cm) rectangles. Cut 8 in BM37AU, 7 in BM37PT, BM37RD and 5 in BM37BE. Total 27 rectangles.

**Border** Down the length of the fabric cut 2 borders 4½in x 51½in (11.5cm x 130.75cm) for the quilt sides and 2 borders 4½in x 43in (11.5cm x 109.25cm) for the quilt top and bottom.

**Binding** Cut 6 strips 2½in (6.5cm) wide across the width of the fabric in SC35.

**Backing** Cut 1 piece 40in x 67in (101.5cm x 170.25cm), 1 piece 40in x 19in (101.5cm x 48.25cm) and 1 piece 28in x 19in (71cm x 48.25cm) in backing fabric.

**MAKING THE BLOCKS**

Use a ¼in (6mm) seam allowance throughout. Refer to the quilt assembly diagram for fabric placement. Lay out each set of patches as shown in block assembly diagram a and join the patches into 4 rows. Join the 4 rows as shown in diagram b to complete the block which can be seen in diagram c. Make 27 blocks.

**MAKING THE QUILT**

Join the blocks into 6 rows as shown in the quilt assembly diagram using the Large Rectangles to fill the ends of the 2nd, 4th and 6th row. Join the rows to make the quilt centre. Join the side borders to the quilt centre, then add a border corner post to each end of the top and bottom borders and then join them to the centre to complete the quilt.

**FINISHING THE QUILT**

Press the quilt top. Seam the backing pieces using a ¼in (6mm) seam allowance to form a piece approx. 58in x 67in (147.25 x 170.25cm). Layer the quilt top, batting and backing and baste together (see page 144). Quilt in a meandering pattern across the surface to the quilt using toning machine quilting thread or alternatively quilt in the ditch to highlight the doll shapes. Trim the quilt edges and attach the binding (see page 145).

# QUILT ASSEMBLY DIAGRAM

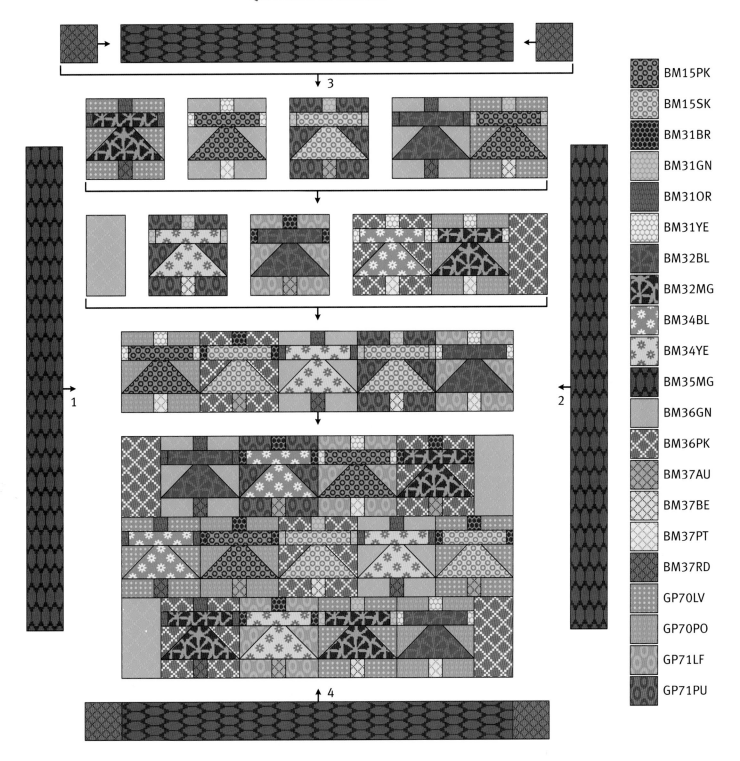

| | |
|---|---|
| BM15PK | |
| BM15SK | |
| BM31BR | |
| BM31GN | |
| BM31OR | |
| BM31YE | |
| BM32BL | |
| BM32MG | |
| BM34BL | |
| BM34YE | |
| BM35MG | |
| BM36GN | |
| BM36PK | |
| BM37AU | |
| BM37BE | |
| BM37PT | |
| BM37RD | |
| GP70LV | |
| GP70PO | |
| GP71LF | |
| GP71PU | |

# traffic jam *

Pauline Smith

These delightful 'Traffic Jam' blocks are made using 2 squares (Templates B and C) and 2 rectangles (Templates D and E) and finish to 6in x 8in (15.25cm x 20.25cm). Each block has 2 fussy cut wheels which are appliquéd using adhesive web, instructions for both sew and non−sew adhesive web can be found in the Patchwork Know How section in the back of the book. The blocks are set into straight rows and the quilt is finished with a simple border. Pauline's traffic jam was obviously on a motorway (highway) as the traffic is all facing the same way, you could of course make your blocks with the vehicles facing in opposite directions for a more urban look!

## SIZE OF QUILT
The finished quilt will measure approx. 50in x 58in (127cm x 147.25cm).

## MATERIALS
**Patchwork Fabrics**
RINGS

| | | |
|---|---|---|
| Sky | BM15SK | ¼yd (25cm) |

SPOT

| | | |
|---|---|---|
| Apple | GP70AL | ⅜yd (35cm) |

ABORIGINAL DOTS

| | | |
|---|---|---|
| Ocean | GP71ON | ¼yd (25cm) |

PLINK

| | | |
|---|---|---|
| Lavender | GP109LV | ¼yd (25cm) |
| Turquoise | GP109TQ | ¼yd (25cm) |

OMBRE

| | | |
|---|---|---|
| Blue | GP117BL | ¼yd (25cm) |
| Pink | GP117PK | ⅜yd (35cm) |

BABAGANOUSH

| | | |
|---|---|---|
| Pink | GP124PK | ¼yd (25cm) |

SHOT COTTON

| | | |
|---|---|---|
| Lavender | SC14 | ⅜yd (35cm) |
| Jade | SC41 | ¼yd (25cm) |
| Lime | SC43 | ¼yd (25cm) |
| Aegean | SC46 | ¼yd (25cm) |
| Clementine | SC80 | ¼yd (25cm) |
| Lipstick | SC82 | ¼yd (25cm) |

WOVEN CATERPILLAR STRIPE

| | | |
|---|---|---|
| Blue | WCS BL | ¼yd (25cm) |

**Border Fabric**
ASIAN CIRCLES

| | | |
|---|---|---|
| Green | GP89GN | ⅞yd (80cm) |

**Appliqué Fabric**
PLINK

| | | |
|---|---|---|
| Red | GP109RD | ¼yd (25cm) |

**Backing Fabric** 3⅜yd (3.1m)
We suggest these fabrics for backing
PLINK, Lavender, GP109TQ or Lavender, GP109LV
BABAGANOUSH, Pink GP124PK

**Binding**
OMBRE
Pink          GP117PK      ½yd (45cm)

**Batting**
58in x 66in (147.25cm x 167.75cm)

**Quilting thread**
Toning machine quilting thread

**You Will Also Need**
Adhesive web for appliqué.

**Templates**

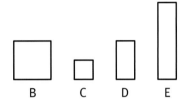

B          C          D          E

This quilt also uses the appliqué shape on page 130.

## CUTTING OUT

Cut the fabric in the order stated, save leftover strips, trim as necessary and use for following templates.
**Template B** Cut 4½in (11.5cm) strips across the width of the fabric, Each strip will give you 8 squares per full width. Cut 9 in GP117PK, 8 in GP124PK, 7 in GP117BL, 6 in GP109LV, 5 in BM15SK and GP109TQ. Total 40 squares.
**Template E** Cut 2½in (6.25cm) strips across the width of the fabric. Cut 8½in x 2½in (21.5cm x 6.25cm) rectangles. Each strip will give you 4 rectangles per full width. Cut 9 in SC14, 6 in SC46, WCS BL, 5 in SC43, SC80, SC82 2 in GP71ON and SC41. Total 40 rectangles.
**Template D** Cut 2½in (6.25cm) strips across the width of the fabric. Cut 4½in x 2½in (11.5cm x 6.25cm) rectangles. Each strip will give you 8 rectangles per full width. Cut 15 in GP70AL, 8 in SC41, 6 in GP71ON, 4 in SC43, SC80 and 3 in SC82. Total 40 rectangles.
**Template C** Cut 2½in (6.25cm) strips across the width of the fabric. Each

strip will give you 16 squares per full width. Cut 15 in GP70AL, 9 in GP117PK, 8 in GP124PK, SC41, 7 in GP117BL, 6 in GP71ON, GP109LV, 5 in BM15SK, GP109TQ, 4 in SC43, SC80 and 3 in SC82. Total 80 squares.

**Borders** Cut 5 strips 5½in (14cm) wide across the width of the fabric, join as necessary and cut 2 side borders 5½in x 58½in (14cm x 148.5cm) and 2 top and bottom borders 5½in x 40½in (14cm x 103cm) in GP89GN.

**Appliqué Shapes** Bond the GP109RD fabric to fusible web in sections and fussy cut a total of 80 circles centred on the circular designs in the fabric. We have provided a template as a guide, but you can vary the size of the wheels as you please.

**Binding** Cut 8 strips 2½in (6.5cm) wide across the width of the fabric in GP92BL.

**Backing** Cut 1 piece 40in x 58in (101.5cm x 147.25cm) and 1 piece 27in x 58in (68.5cm x 147.25cm) in backing fabric.

### MAKING THE BLOCKS
Use a ¼in (6mm) seam allowance throughout. Refer to the quilt assembly diagram for fabric placement. Lay out each block, first join the 2 template C squares as shown in diagram a. Next take the template D rectangle and template B square and join to the first section as shown in diagram b. It's at this stage you can reverse the direction of the vehicle by swapping the position of templates D and B. Finally add the template E rectangle to the bottom of the pieced section to form the road as shown in diagram c. Make a total of 40 blocks.

### APPLIQUÉ
Full instructions for using adhesive web for appliqué can be found in the Patchwork Know How section on page 143. Remove the backing paper from the appliqué shapes and position carefully as shown in diagram d. The rear wheel should be positioned ⅝in (1.5cm) from the raw edge to the right of the wheel edge. Bond the shapes into place according to the manufacturer's instructions and stitch using a blanket or fine zigzag stitch if necessary.

### MAKING THE QUILT
Join the blocks into 8 rows of 5 blocks, then join the rows to complete the quilt centre. Add the top and bottom borders, then the side borders as shown in the quilt assembly diagram.

### FINISHING THE QUILT
Press the quilt top. Seam the backing pieces using a ¼in (6mm) seam allowance to form a piece approx. 58in x 66in (147.25cm x 167.75cm). Layer the quilt top, batting and backing and baste together (see page 144). Machine quilt in the ditch along all the seams between the blocks and around each lorry to highlight the shape. Trim the quilt edges and attach the binding (see page 145).

**BLOCK ASSEMBLY DIAGRAMS**

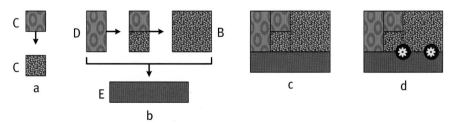

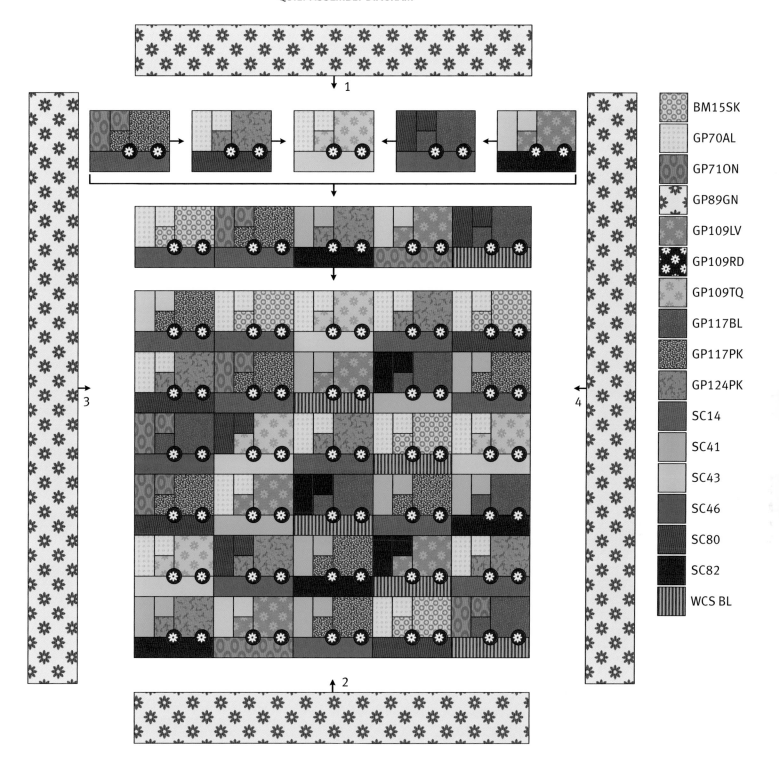

BM15SK
GP70AL
GP71ON
GP89GN
GP109LV
GP109RD
GP109TQ
GP117BL
GP117PK
GP124PK
SC14
SC41
SC43
SC46
SC80
SC82
WCS BL

# swirling petals ✴✴✴

Mary Mashuta

The 'swirling petals' blocks in this quilt are made using 3 curved edge patch shapes (Templates PP, QQ and RR). The PP shapes form the block centres, the QQ shapes form the background and the RR shapes are the 'petals'. The blocks finish to 10½in (26.5cm). The blocks are straight set into rows and surrounded with a simple border with corner posts.

## SIZE OF QUILT
The finished quilt will measure approx. 67½in x 88½in (171.5cm x 224.75cm)

## MATERIALS
### Patchwork Fabrics
GUINEA FLOWER
| | | |
|---|---|---|
| Turquoise | GP59TQ | ⅜yd (35cm) |

SPOT
| | | |
|---|---|---|
| Green | GP70GN | 1yd (90cm) |
| Sapphire | GP70SP | 1yd (90cm) |

PLINK
| | | |
|---|---|---|
| Lavender | GP109LV | 1⅞yd (1.7m) |
| Magenta | GP109MG | 2yd (1.85m) |

### Border Fabrics
RINGS
| | | |
|---|---|---|
| Green | BM15GN | ⅜yd (35cm) |

RADIATION
| | | |
|---|---|---|
| Blue | GP115BL | 1¾yd (1.6m) |

### Backing Fabric 5¾yd (5.25m)
We suggest these fabrics for backing
RINGS Blue, BM15BL
PLINK Turquoise, GP109TQ or Green, GP109GN

### Binding
OMBRE
| | | |
|---|---|---|
| Blue | GP117BL | ¾yd (70cm) |

### Batting
75in x 96in (190.5cm x 243.75cm)

### Quilting thread
Toning and light blue or yellow machine quilting thread

### Templates

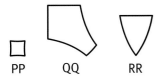

## CUTTING OUT
Please read the cutting instructions carefully as some pieces are fussy cut. Cutting layouts are provided for templates QQ and RR.

**Template PP** Fussy cut 35 in GP59TQ centring on the floral motifs in the fabric design. Making a template from transparent template plastic will help with this. Mary suggests cutting a second set of 35 template PP shapes from the leftover fabric to reinforce this shape. If you decide to do this, baste one of these to the wrong side of each of the fussy cut shapes.

**Template QQ** Cut 5⅞in (15cm) strips across the width of the fabric. Each strip will give you 7 patches per row, see the cutting layout for template QQ. Cut 72 in GP109MG and 68 in GP109LV. Total 140 patches.

**Template RR** Cut 4⅞in (12.5cm) strips across the width of the fabric. Each strip will give you 13 patches per row, see the cutting layout for template RR. Cut 72 in GP70GN and 68 in GP70SP. Total 140 patches.

**Border** Cut 7 strips 8in (20.25cm) across the width of the fabric, join as necessary and cut 2 borders 8in x 74in (20.25cm x 188cm) for the quilt sides and 2 borders 8in x 53in (20.25cm and 134.5cm) in GP115BL.

**Border Corner Posts** Cut 4 squares 8in x 8in (20.25cm x 20.25cm) in BM15GN.

**Binding** Cut 9 strips 2½in (6.5cm) wide across the width of the fabric in GP117BL.

**Backing** Cut 1 piece 40in x 96in (101.5cm x 243.75cm) and 1 piece 36in x 96in (91.5 x 243.75cm) in backing fabric.

## MAKING THE BLOCKS
Use a ¼in (6mm) seam allowance throughout, this is particularly important for these blocks to lay flat. The blocks are made in 2 colourways as shown in the quilt assembly diagram. Make a second set of templates, this time using the sewing lines. Mark your patches with the sewing lines and register marks with a washable marker pen or pencil. Match your patches with the concave curve (curve goes in) on top and the convex curve (curve goes out) beneath and use 3 pins along the length of the curve. The curves in these blocks are gentle and should not be difficult to ease gently into place as you sew. When stitching the curved seams start sewing with a backstitch ¼in (6mm) from the edge and finish ¼in (6mm) short of the raw edge and backstitch to secure. Finger press the pieces as you go but wait to press the seams with your iron until the block is complete. Make a total of 35 blocks as shown in block assembly diagrams a and b, the finished block can be seen in diagram c.

> **Mary says:**
> The pressing for these blocks is important, press the seams between the QQ shapes and the RR petals towards the QQ, then press the seams between the PP centres and QQ shapes towards the QQ shapes.

### CUTTING LAYOUT FOR TEMPLATE QQ

### CUTTING LAYOUT FOR TEMPLATE RR

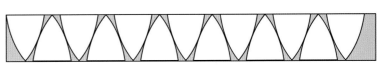

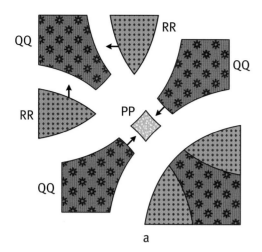
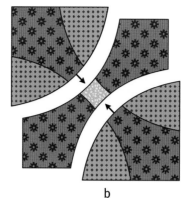

a                                    b                                    c

## MAKING THE QUILT

Lay out the blocks alternating the 2 colourway throughout as shown in the quilt assembly diagram. Join into 7 rows of 5 blocks. Join the blocks to complete the quilt centre. Add the side borders to the quilt centre. Join a corner post to each end of the top and bottom borders and join to the quilt centre to complete the quilt.

## FINISHING THE QUILT

Press the quilt top. Seam the backing pieces using a ¼in (6mm) seam allowance to form a piece approx. 75in x 96in (190.5cm x 243.75cm). Layer the quilt top, batting and backing and baste together (see page 144). Using toning machine quilting thread quilt in the ditch between the blocks and in the block and border seams. Using light blue or yellow quilting thread quilt the blocks and borders as shown in the quilting diagram. Trim the quilt edges and attach the binding (see page 145).

**QUILTING DIAGRAM**

## Mary says:

Many machines or walking feet have a seam guide which can be set so that you can stitch an even ¾in (2cm) offset from the seams in this quilt, as shown in the quilting diagram. Be aware that stitching can often continue from one block to the next.

# QUILT ASSEMBLY DIAGRAM

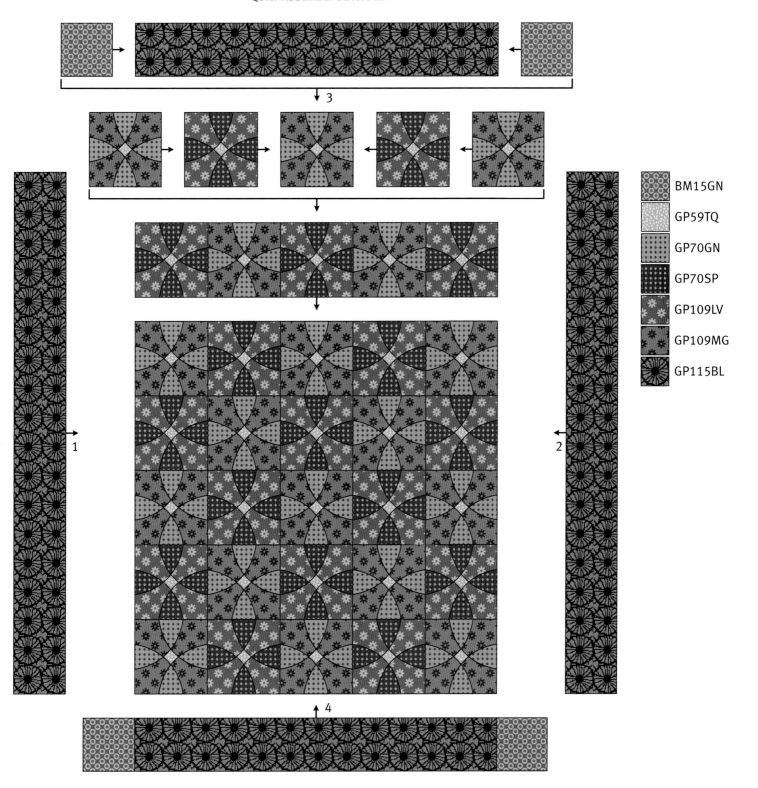

BM15GN

GP59TQ

GP70GN

GP70SP

GP109LV

GP109MG

GP115BL

1

2

3

4

# meadow pathways **

### Sally Davis

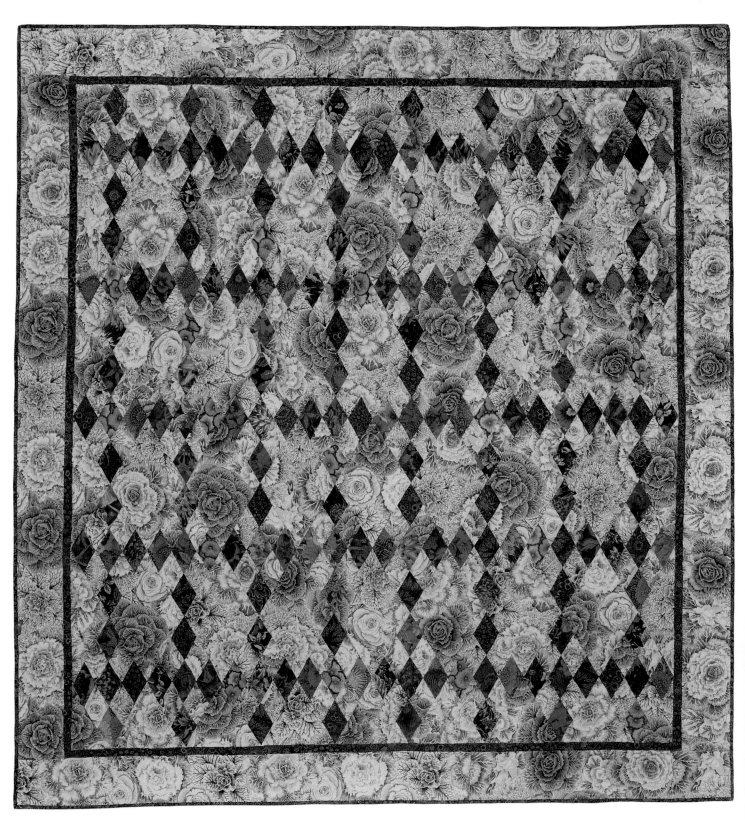

This vibrant quilt is made using 2 sizes of 60 degree diamonds (Template WW and XX) with 3 triangles (Templates YY, ZZ and AAA & Reverse AAA) used to fill the quilt edges and corners. The smaller diamonds are pieced into blocks and alternated in diagonal rows with the larger diamonds. The quilt is completed with a simple narrow inner border and a wider outer border. Some of the templates for this quilt are large and need to be traced on to folded paper to complete the shapes.

## SIZE OF QUILT
The finished quilt will measure approx. 86in x 92in (218.5cm x 233.75cm).

## MATERIALS
### Patchwork and Border Fabrics
MILLEFIORE
Blue          GP92BL      ¾yd (70cm)
GRANDIOSE
Turquoise     PJ13TQ      ¼yd (25cm)
BEGONIA LEAVES
Cobalt        PJ18CB      ¼yd (25cm)
RAMBLING ROSE
Blue          PJ34BL      ¼yd (25cm)
JAPANESE CHRYSANTHEMUM
Purple        PJ41PU      ⅜yd (35cm)
PETUNIAS
Blue          PJ50BL      ⅜yd (35cm)
Green         PJ50GN      ⅛yd (15cm)
BRASSICA
Green         PJ51GN      6¾yd (6.2m)
PICOTTE POPPIES
Turquoise     PJ52TQ      ¼yd (25cm)
GRANDIFLORA
Purple        PJ53PU      ¼yd (25cm)
CACTUS DAHLIAS
Blue          PJ54BL      ¼yd (25cm)
LACY
Blue          PJ58BL      ⅜yd (35cm)

Backing Fabric 7⅛yd (6.5m)
We suggest these fabrics for backing
LOTUS LEAF Blue, GP29BL
PETUNIAS Blue, GP50BL
BRASSICA Blue, PJ51BL

Binding
MILLEFIORE
Blue          GP92BL      ⅞yd (80cm)

Batting
92in x 100in (233.75cm x 254cm)

Quilting thread
Toning machine quilting thread

Templates

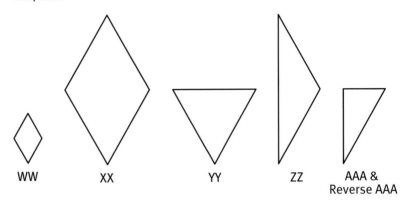

WW     XX     YY     ZZ     AAA &
                                   Reverse AAA

## CUTTING OUT
To make templates for the larger shapes, XX, YY and ZZ use large sheets of paper (A3) or join smaller pieces with tape. For template XX you will need to fold the paper very carefully down the centre vertically then horizontally. Place the edges of template XX to the folds, trace the shape and cut out. Open out for the complete template. Trace the completed shape into template plastic and mark on the seam line. For templates YY and ZZ use the same technique on a single fold of paper. Cut the fabric in the order stated to prevent waste.

**Outer Borders** Cut 9 strips 6½in (16.5cm) wide across the width of the fabric in PJ51GN. Join as necessary and cut 2 outer borders 6½in x 86½in (16.5cm x 219.75cm) for the quilt top and bottom and 2 outer borders 6½in x 80½in (16.5cm x 204.5cm) for the quilt sides.

**Inner Borders** Cut 8 strips 1½in (3.75cm) wide across the width of the fabric in GP92BL. Join as necessary and cut 2 inner borders 1½in x 78½in (3.75cm x 199.5cm) for the quilt sides and 2 inner borders 1½in x 74½in (3.75cm x 189.25cm) for the quilt top and bottom.

**Template XX** Cut 8¼in (21cm) strips across the width of the fabric, Each strip will give you 3 diamonds per full width. Cut 28 in PJ51GN.

**Template YY** Cut 8½in (21.5cm) strips across the width of the fabric, Each strip will give you 7 triangles per full width. Cut 14 in PJ51GN.

**Template ZZ** Cut 5in (12.75cm) strips across the width of the fabric, Each strip will give you 3 triangles per full width. Align the long side of the template with the cut edge of the strip, this will ensure that the long side of the triangles will not have a bias edge. Cut 8 in PJ51GN.

## BLOCK ASSEMBLY DIAGRAMS

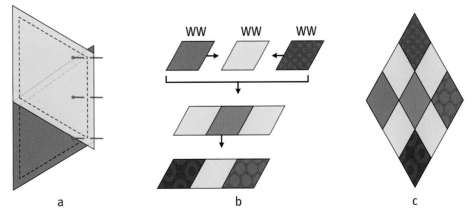

a          b          c

123

**Template AAA & Reverse AAA** Cut a 5¼in (13.25cm) strip across the width of the fabric. Cut 2 in PJ51GN. Reverse the template by flipping it over and cut 2 more in PJ51GN. Total 4 triangles.

**Template WW** Cut 3⅛in (8cm) strips across the width of the fabric, Each strip will give you 10 diamonds per full width. Cut 160 in PJ51GN, 29 in PJ50BL, 23 in PJ41PU, 22 in GP92BL, 21 in PJ58BL, 20 in PJ52TQ, PJ53PU, 18 in PJ34BL, 16 in PJ18CB, 13 in PJ54BL 12 in PJ13TQ and 6 in PJ50GN. Total 360 diamonds.

**Binding** 10 strips 2½in (6.5cm) wide across the width of the fabric in GP92BL.

**Backing** Cut 2 pieces 40in x 92in (101.5cm x 233.75cm), 2 pieces 40in x 21in (101.5cm x 53.25cm) and 1 piece 21in x 13in (53.25cm x 33cm) in backing fabric.

### MAKING THE BLOCKS

Use a ¼in (6mm) seam allowance throughout. Refer to the quilt assembly diagram for fabric placement. Lay out the first block and separate into rows as shown in block assembly diagram b. Take the first 2 diamonds and place right sides together. You will need to offset the diamonds so that the sewing lines intersect at the correct position as shown in diagram a. Join the diamonds into 3 rows, then join the rows to complete the block, again offsetting the seams in the same way as before. Make a total of 40 blocks.

### Sally says:

If this is the first time you have sewn diamond shapes you may wish to trace a second template on the dotted line and use it to mark the sewing lines onto the first few fabric diamonds. Once you have sewn a few the offset positioning becomes routine.

### MAKING THE QUILT

Lay out the blocks alternating with the template XX diamonds as shown in the quilt assembly diagram. Fill the quilt edges and corners with the triangle shapes as shown. Separate into diagonal rows and using the same offsetting technique stitch into rows. Join the rows to complete the quilt centre. Add the side inner borders, followed by the top and bottom inner borders. Add the outer border in the same manner as shown in the quilt assembly diagram.

### FINISHING THE QUILT

Press the quilt top. Seam the backing pieces using a ¼in (6mm) seam allowance to form a piece approx. 92in x 100in (233.75cm x 254cm). Layer the quilt top, batting and backing and baste together (see page 144). Using toning machine quilting thread free motion quilt in an all over floral design following motifs in the fabric designs if you wish. Trim the quilt edges and attach the binding (see page 145).

# QUILT ASSEMBLY DIAGRAM

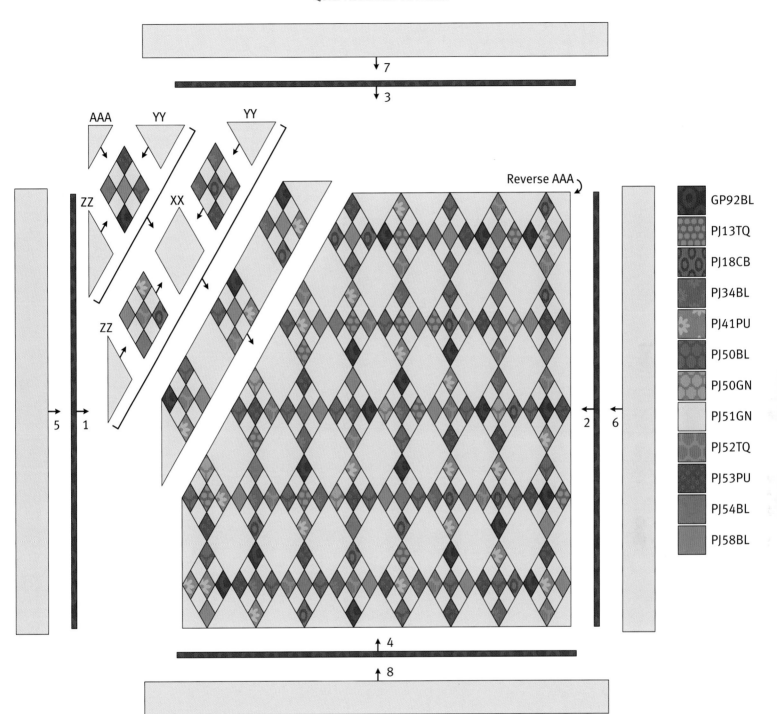

| | |
|---|---|
| | GP92BL |
| | PJ13TQ |
| | PJ18CB |
| | PJ34BL |
| | PJ41PU |
| | PJ50BL |
| | PJ50GN |
| | PJ51GN |
| | PJ52TQ |
| | PJ53PU |
| | PJ54BL |
| | PJ58BL |

# blue haze *

## Pauline Smith

The large blocks in this quilt are created using a single triangle shape (Template A) and finish to 30in (76.25cm) square. As the blocks are so large, it is easier to make each block in 4 quarter sections. The blocks are then joined into simple straight set rows.

## SIZE OF QUILT
The finished quilt will measure approx. 90in x 90in (228.5cm x 228.5cm).

## MATERIALS
### Patchwork Fabrics
RINGS
| | | |
|---|---|---|
| Sky | BM15SK | 1⅛yd (1m) |

CABBAGE AND ROSE
| | | |
|---|---|---|
| Blue | GP38BL | ½yd (45cm) |

SPOT
| | | |
|---|---|---|
| Green | GP70GN | 1yd (90cm) |
| Periwinkle | GP70PE | ½yd (45cm) |

MILLEFIORE
| | | |
|---|---|---|
| Blue | GP92BL | 1⅛yd (1m) |

PLINK
| | | |
|---|---|---|
| Lavender | GP109LV | 1yd (90cm) |
| Turquoise | GP109TQ | 1½yd (1.4m) |

OMBRE
| | | |
|---|---|---|
| Blue | GP117BL | 1½yd (1.4m) |

TILE FLOWERS
| | | |
|---|---|---|
| Turquoise | GP125TQ | 2yd (1.8m) |

BRASSICA
| | | |
|---|---|---|
| Blue | PJ51BL | 1yd (90cm) |

**Backing Fabric** 7½yd (6.9m)
We suggest these fabrics for backing
BRASSICA Blue, PJ51BL
CABBAGE AND ROSE Blue, GP38BL
PLINK Turquoise, GP109TQ

## Binding
OMBRE
| | | |
|---|---|---|
| Blue | GP117BL | ⅞yd (80cm) |

## Batting
98in x 98in (249cm x 249cm)

## Quilting thread
Blue perlé embroidery thread

## Templates

A

## CUTTING OUT
Template A Cut 5⅞in (15cm) strips across the width of the fabric, each strip will give you 12 triangles per full width. Cut 5⅞in (15cm) squares, then cut each square diagonally to form 2 triangles using the template as a guide. Handle the triangles carefully as the long edge will be on the bias and stretchy. Cut 126 triangles in GP125TQ, 90 in GP109TQ, GP117BL, 72 in BM15SK, GP92BL, 54 in GP70GN, GP109LV, PJ51BL, 18 in GP38BL and GP70PE. Total 648 triangles.

**Binding** Cut 8 strips 2½in (6.5cm) wide across the width of the fabric in GP92BL.

**Backing** Cut 2 pieces 40in x 98in (101.5cm x 249cm), 2 pieces 40in x 19in (101.5cm x 48.25cm) and 1 piece 19in x 19in (48.25cm x 48.25cm) in backing fabric.

## MAKING THE BLOCKS
Use a ¼in (6mm) seam allowance throughout. Refer to the quilt assembly diagram for fabric placement. First join the triangles in pairs to form squares as shown in diagram a. Handle the triangles carefully and take care not to stretch the diagonal seam as you sew. Next lay out the block and join into 4 sections as shown in diagram b. Join the 4 quarter sections to form the block as shown in diagram c. The finished block can be seen in diagram d. Make a total of 9 identical blocks.

## MAKING THE QUILT
Join the blocks into 3 rows of 3 blocks, then join the rows to complete the quilt top.

### BLOCK ASSEMBLY DIAGRAMS

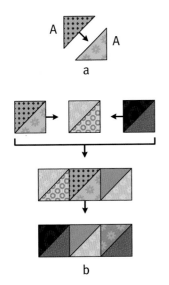

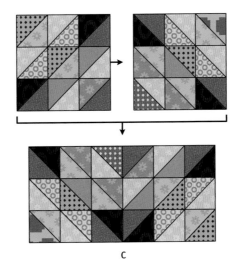

d

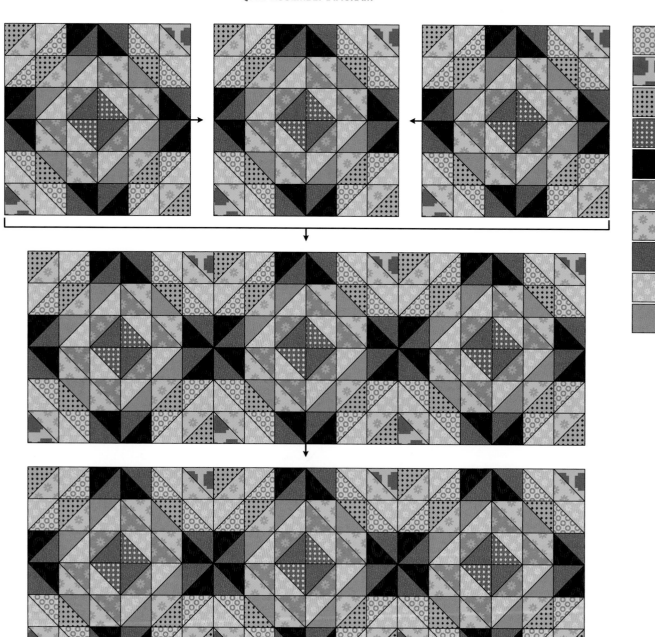

| | |
|---|---|
| | BM15SK |
| | GP38BL |
| | GP70GN |
| | GP70PE |
| | GP92BL |
| | GP109LV |
| | GP109TQ |
| | GP117BL |
| | GP125TQ |
| | PJ51BL |

**FINISHING THE QUILT**

Press the quilt top. Seam the backing pieces using a ¼in (6mm) seam allowance to form a piece approx. 98in x 98in (249cm x 249cm). Layer the quilt top, batting and backing and baste together (see page 144). Quilt in the ditch along all the diagonal seams using blue perlé embroidery thread. Trim the quilt edges and attach the binding (see page 145).

# templates

Please refer to the individual instructions for the templates required for each quilt as some templates are used in several projects. The arrows on the templates should be lined up with the straight grain of the fabric, which runs either along the selvedge or at 90 degrees to the selvedge. Following the marked grain lines is important to prevent patches having bias edges along block and quilt edges which can cause distortion. In some quilts the arrows also denote stripe direction.

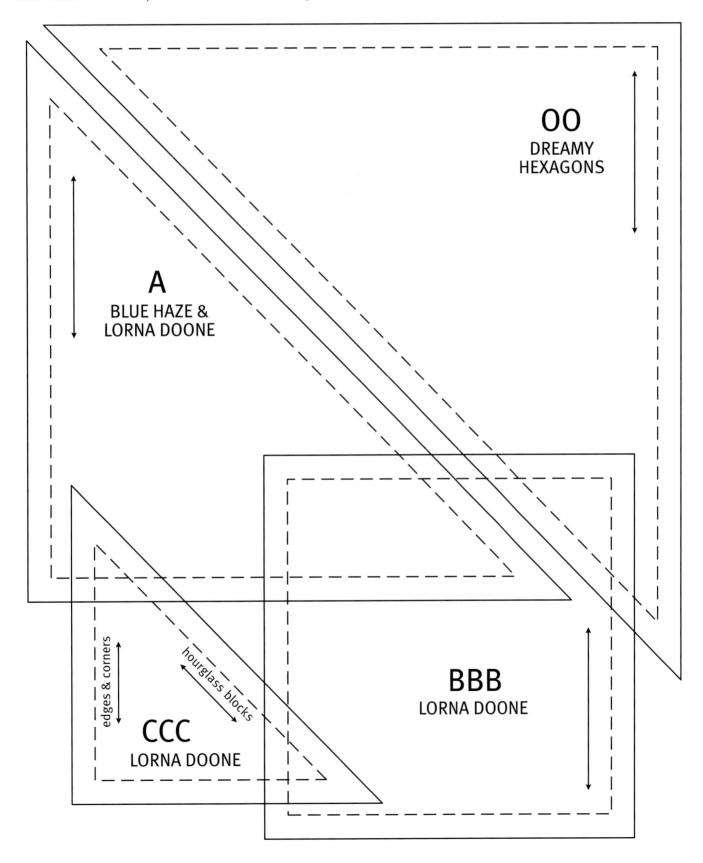

OO
DREAMY
HEXAGONS

A
BLUE HAZE &
LORNA DOONE

edges & corners

hourglass blocks

BBB
LORNA DOONE

CCC
LORNA DOONE

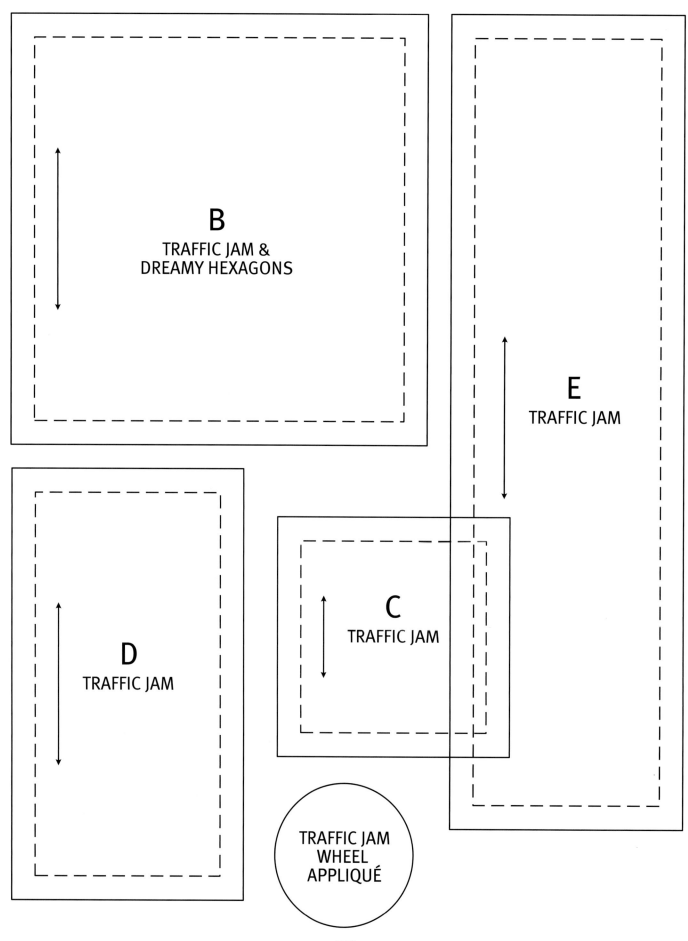

B

TRAFFIC JAM &
DREAMY HEXAGONS

E

TRAFFIC JAM

D

TRAFFIC JAM

C

TRAFFIC JAM

TRAFFIC JAM
WHEEL
APPLIQUÉ

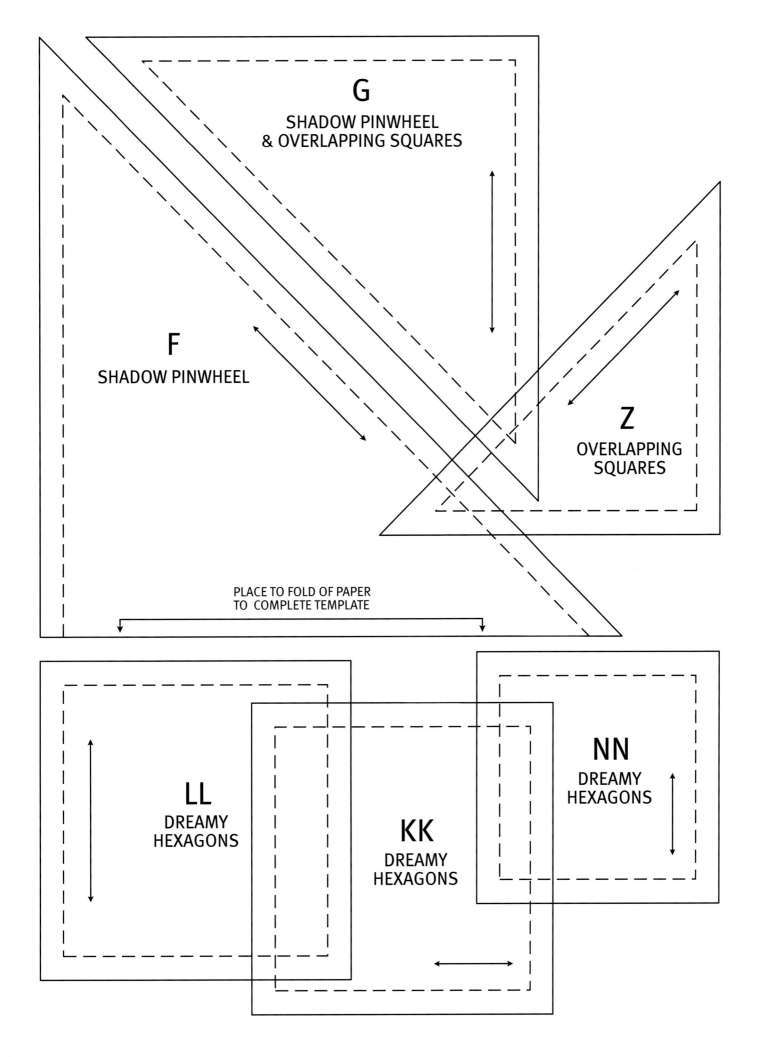

G
SHADOW PINWHEEL
& OVERLAPPING SQUARES

F
SHADOW PINWHEEL

Z
OVERLAPPING
SQUARES

PLACE TO FOLD OF PAPER
TO COMPLETE TEMPLATE

LL
DREAMY
HEXAGONS

KK
DREAMY
HEXAGONS

NN
DREAMY
HEXAGONS

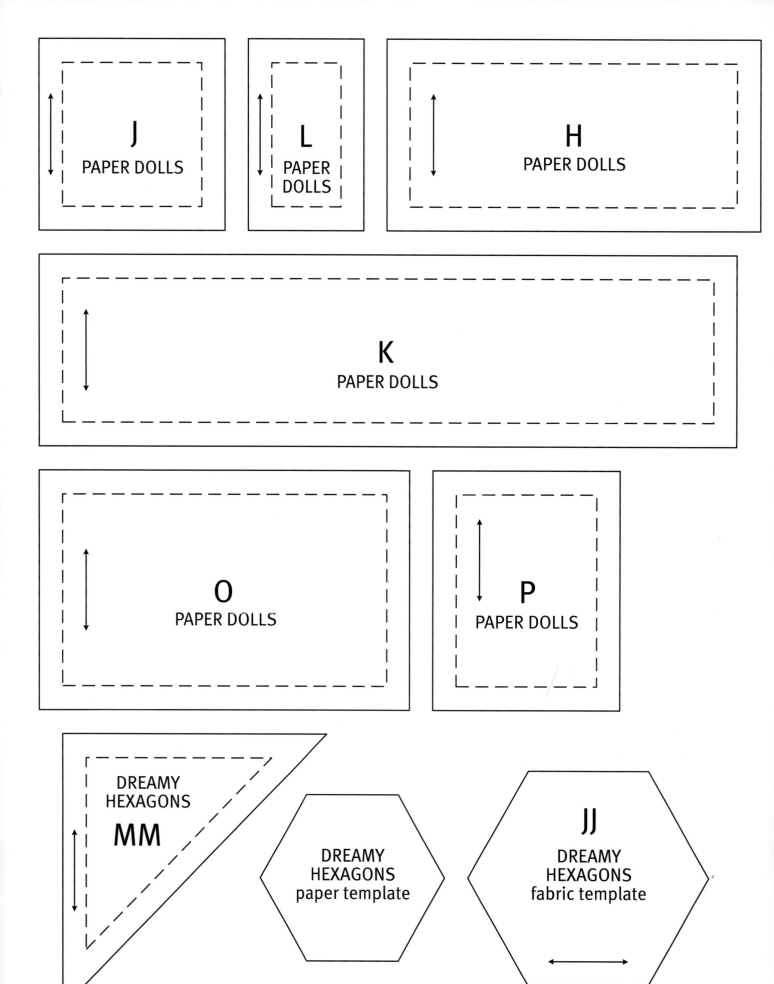

J
PAPER DOLLS

L
PAPER
DOLLS

H
PAPER DOLLS

K
PAPER DOLLS

O
PAPER DOLLS

P
PAPER DOLLS

DREAMY
HEXAGONS
MM

DREAMY
HEXAGONS
paper template

JJ
DREAMY
HEXAGONS
fabric template

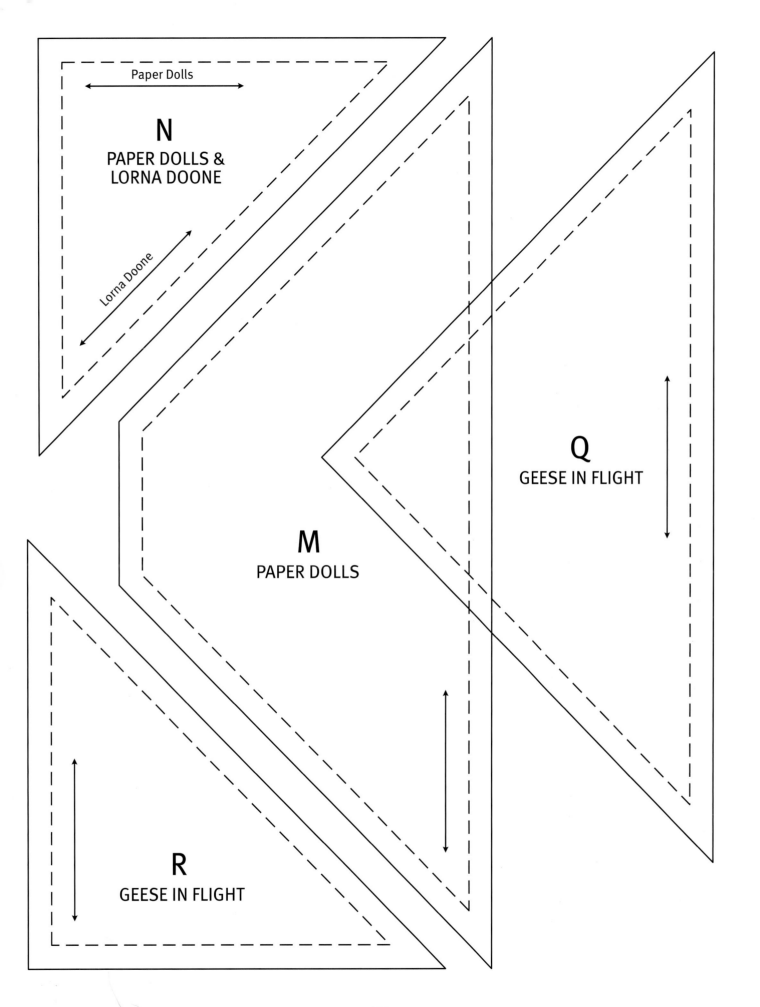

N
PAPER DOLLS &
LORNA DOONE

Paper Dolls

Lorna Doone

M
PAPER DOLLS

Q
GEESE IN FLIGHT

R
GEESE IN FLIGHT

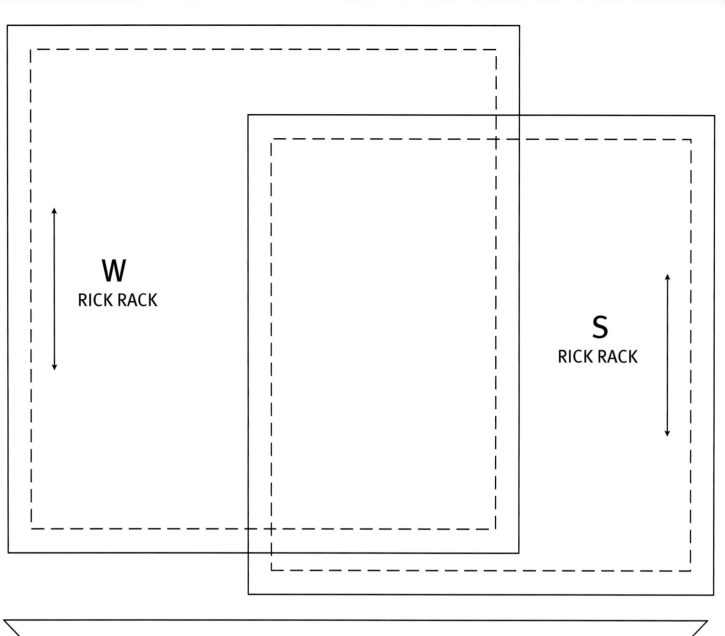

W
RICK RACK

S
RICK RACK

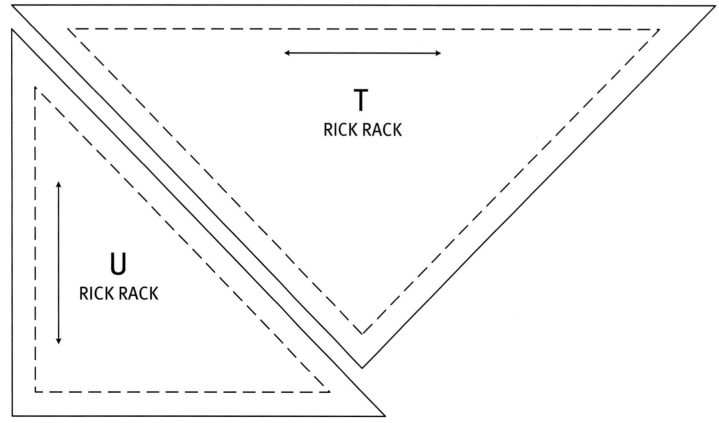

T
RICK RACK

U
RICK RACK

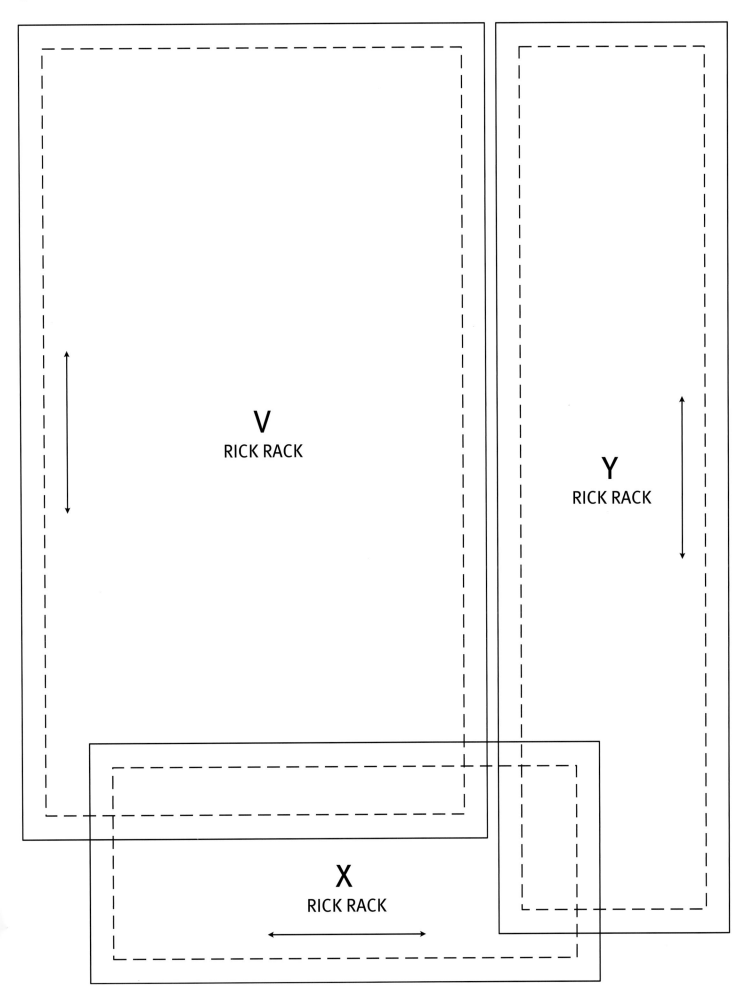

V
RICK RACK

Y
RICK RACK

X
RICK RACK

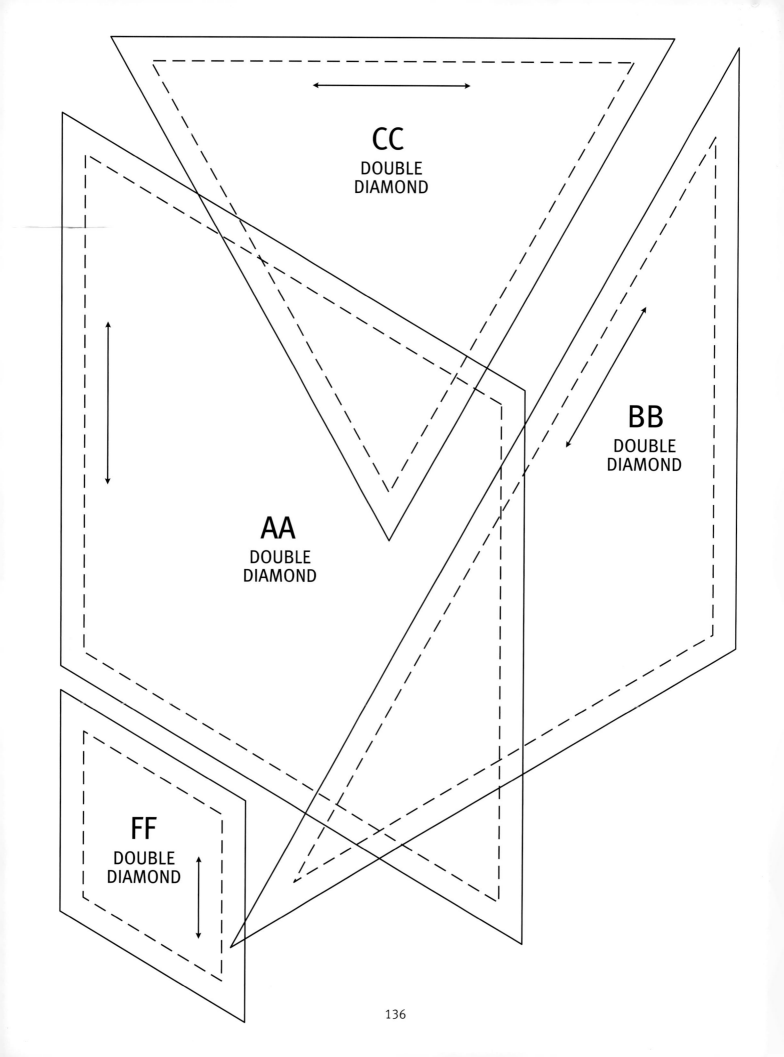

CC
DOUBLE
DIAMOND

BB
DOUBLE
DIAMOND

AA
DOUBLE
DIAMOND

FF
DOUBLE
DIAMOND

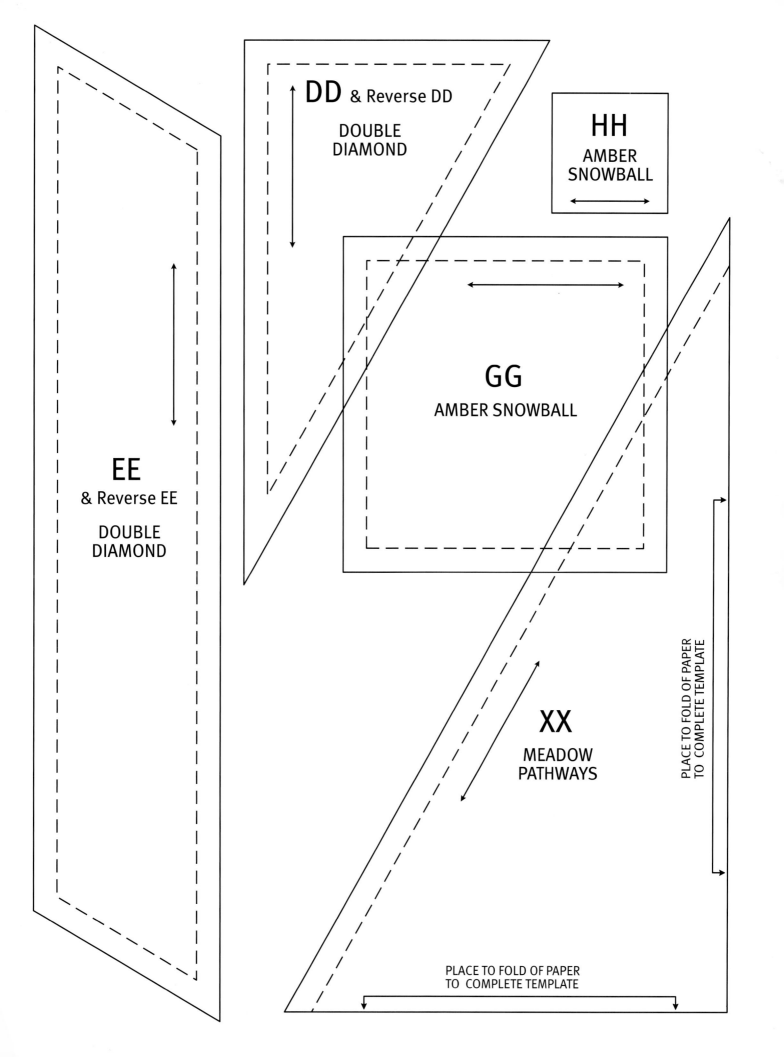

**DD** & Reverse DD

DOUBLE
DIAMOND

**HH**
AMBER
SNOWBALL

**GG**

AMBER SNOWBALL

**EE**

& Reverse EE

DOUBLE
DIAMOND

**XX**

MEADOW
PATHWAYS

PLACE TO FOLD OF PAPER
TO COMPLETE TEMPLATE

PLACE TO FOLD OF PAPER
TO COMPLETE TEMPLATE

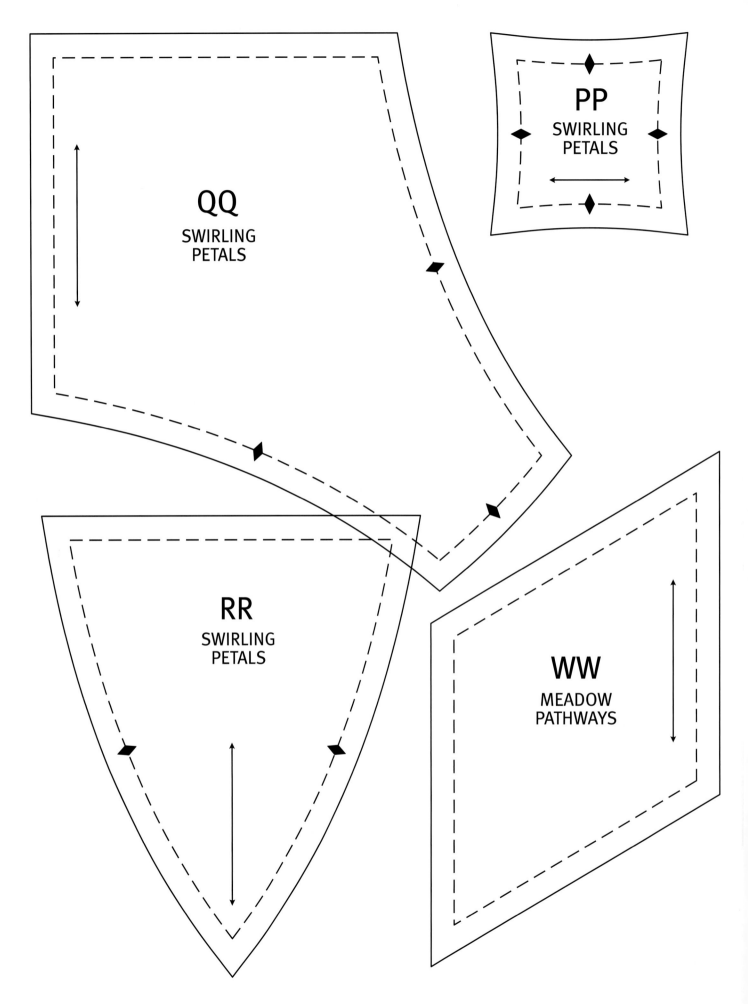

QQ
SWIRLING
PETALS

PP
SWIRLING
PETALS

RR
SWIRLING
PETALS

WW
MEADOW
PATHWAYS

138

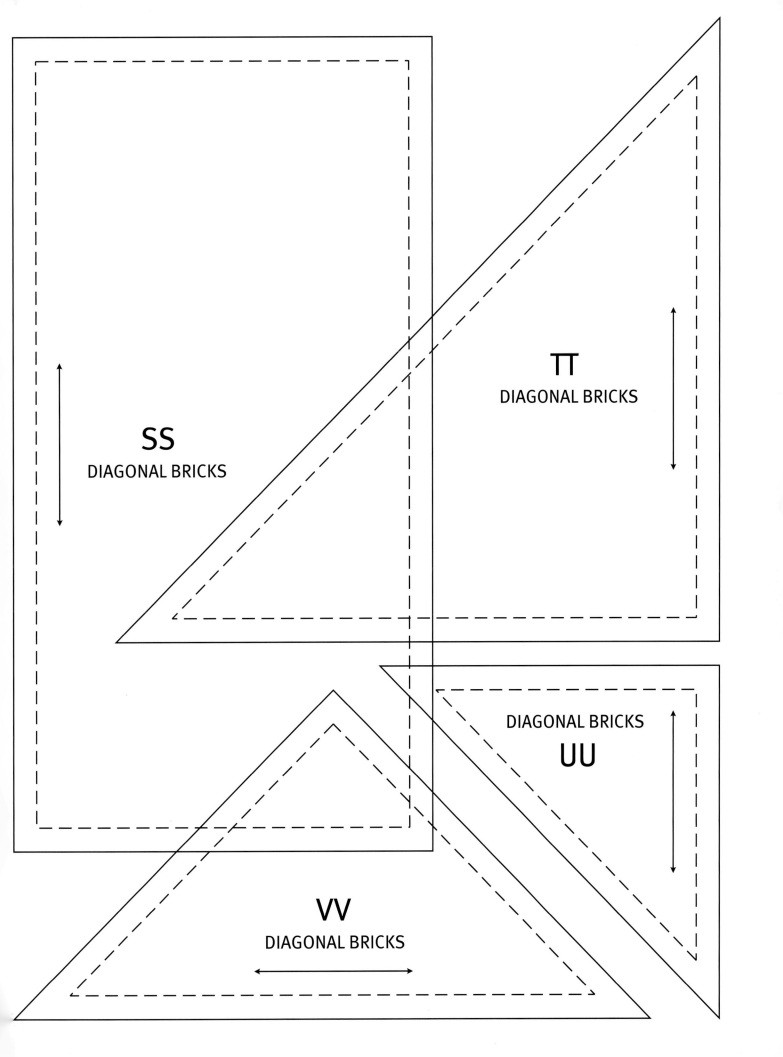

SS
DIAGONAL BRICKS

TT
DIAGONAL BRICKS

DIAGONAL BRICKS
UU

VV
DIAGONAL BRICKS

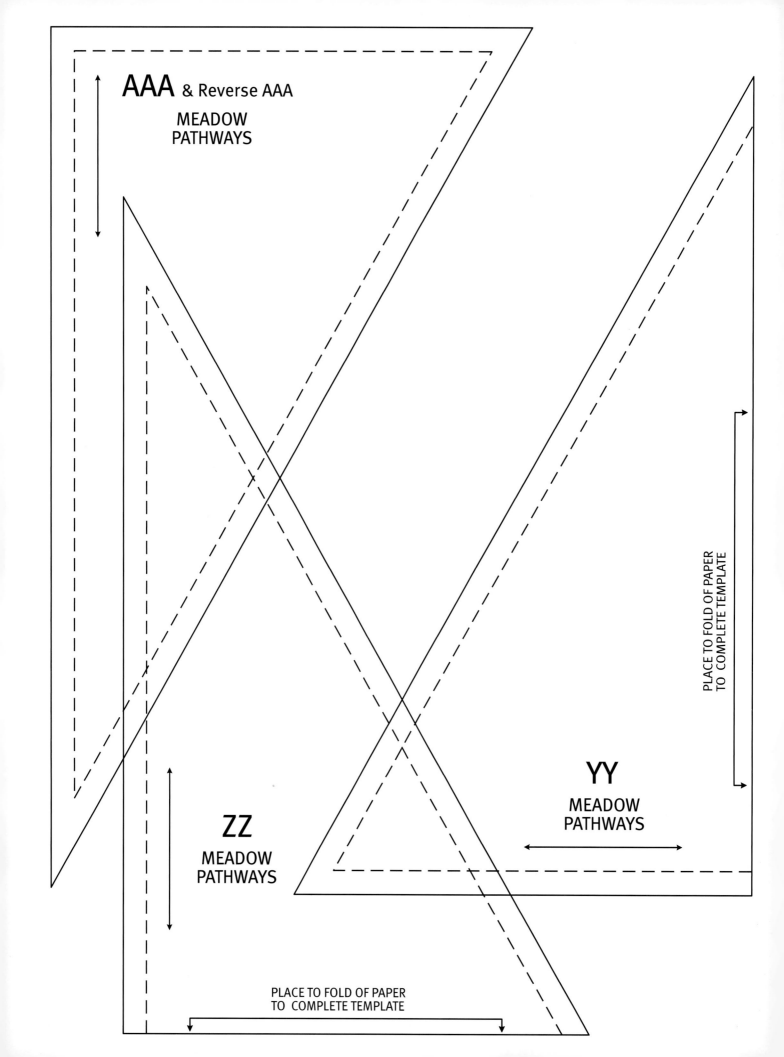

**AAA** & Reverse AAA

MEADOW
PATHWAYS

**ZZ**

MEADOW
PATHWAYS

**YY**

MEADOW
PATHWAYS

PLACE TO FOLD OF PAPER
TO COMPLETE TEMPLATE

PLACE TO FOLD OF PAPER
TO COMPLETE TEMPLATE

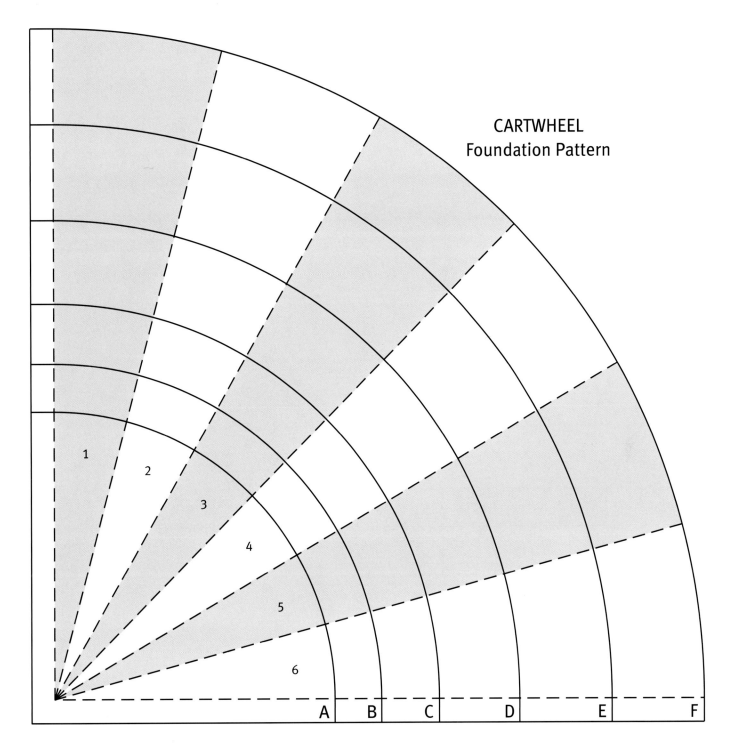

CARTWHEEL
Foundation Pattern

1
2
3
4
5
6

A  B  C  D  E  F

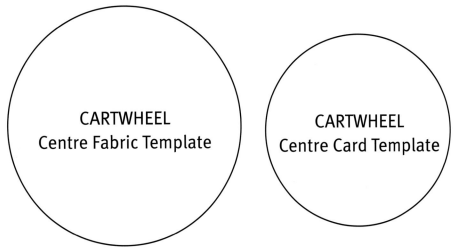

CARTWHEEL
Centre Fabric Template

CARTWHEEL
Centre Card Template

# patchwork know-how

These instructions are intended for the novice quilt maker, providing the basic information needed to make the projects in this book, along with some useful tips.

## EXPERIENCE RATINGS
\* Easy, straightforward, suitable for a beginner.
\*\* Suitable for the average patchwork and quilter.
\*\*\* For the more experienced patchwork and quilter.

## ABOUT THE FABRICS
The fabrics used for the quilts in this book are from Kaffe Fassett Collective. The first two letters of the fabric codes denote the designer:
**GP** is the code for the Kaffe Fassett collection
**PJ** is the code for the Philip Jacobs collection
**BM** is the code for the Brandon Mably collection.

## PREPARING THE FABRIC
Prewash all new fabrics before you begin, to ensure that there will be no uneven shrinkage and no bleeding of colours when the finished quilt is laundered. Press the fabric whilst it is still damp to return crispness to it. All fabric requirements in this book are calculated on a 40in (101.5cm) usable fabric width, to allow for shrinkage and selvedge removal.

## MAKING TEMPLATES
Transparent template plastic is the best material to use: it is durable and allows you to see the fabric and select certain motifs. You can also use thin stiff cardboard.

### Templates for machine piecing
1 Trace off the actual–sized template provided either directly on to template plastic, or tracing paper, and then on to thin cardboard. Use a ruler to help you trace off the straight cutting line, dotted seam line and grain lines.
   Some of the templates in this book were too large to print complete. Transfer the template onto the fold of a large sheet of paper, cut out and open out for the full template.
2 Cut out the traced off template using a craft knife, a ruler and a self–healing cutting mat.
3 Punch holes in the corners of the template, at each point on the seam line, using a hole punch.

### Templates for hand piecing
• Make a template as for machine piecing, but do not trace off the cutting line. Use the dotted seam line as the outer edge of the template.

• This template allows you to draw the seam lines directly on to the fabric. The seam allowances can then be cut by eye around the patch.

## CUTTING THE FABRIC
On the individual instructions for each project, you will find a summary of all the patch shapes used.
   Always mark and cut out any border and binding strips first, followed by the largest patch shapes and finally the smallest ones, to make the most efficient use of your fabric. The border and binding strips are best cut using a rotary cutter.

### Rotary cutting
Rotary cut strips are usually cut across the fabric from selvedge to selvedge, but some projects may vary, so please read through all the instructions before you start cutting the fabrics.

1 Before beginning to cut, press out any folds or creases in the fabric. If you are cutting a large piece of fabric, you will need to fold it several times to fit the cutting mat. When there is only a single fold, place the fold facing you. If the fabric is too wide to be folded only once, fold it concertina-style until it fits your mat. A small rotary cutter with a sharp blade will cut up to six layers of fabric; a large cutter up to eight layers.

2 To ensure that your cut strips are straight and even, the folds must be placed exactly parallel to the straight edges of the fabric and along a line on the cutting mat.

3 Place a plastic ruler over the raw edge of the fabric, overlapping it about ½in (1.25cm). Make sure that the ruler is at right angles to both the straight edges and the fold to ensure that you cut along the straight grain. Press down on the ruler and wheel the cutter away from you along the edge of the ruler.

4 Open out the fabric to check the edge. Don't worry if it's not perfectly straight – a little wiggle will not show when the quilt is stitched together. Re-fold fabric, then place the ruler over the trimmed edge, aligning the edge with the markings on the ruler that match the correct strip width. Cut strip along the edge of the ruler.

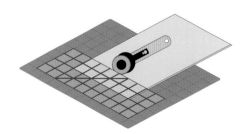

## USING TEMPLATES
The most efficient way to cut out templates is by first rotary cutting a strip of fabric to the width stated for your template, and then marking off your templates along the strip, edge to edge at the required angle. This method leaves hardly any waste and gives a random effect to your patches.
   A less efficient method is to 'fussy cut' them, where the templates are cut individually by placing them on particular motifs or stripes, to create special effects. Although this method is more wasteful, it yields very interesting results.

1 Place the template face down, on the wrong side of the fabric, with the grain-line arrow following the straight grain of the fabric, if indicated. Be careful though – check with your individual instructions, as some instructions may ask you to cut patches on varying grains.

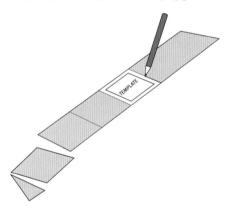

2 Hold the template firmly in place and draw around it with a sharp pencil or crayon, marking in the corner dots or seam lines. To save fabric, position patches close together or even touching. Don't worry if outlines positioned on the straight grain when drawn on striped fabrics do not always match the stripes when cut – this will add a degree of visual excitement to the patchwork!

3 Once you've drawn all the pieces needed, you are ready to cut the fabric, with either a rotary cutter and ruler or a pair of sharp sewing scissors.

## BASIC HAND AND MACHINE PIECING
Patches can be stitched together by hand or machine. Machine stitching is quicker, but hand assembly allows you to carry your patches around with you and work on them in every spare moment. The choice is yours. For techniques that are new to you, practise on scrap pieces of fabric until you feel confident.

## Machine piecing

Follow the quilt instructions for the order in which to piece the individual patchwork blocks and then assemble the blocks together in rows.

1 Seam lines are not marked on the fabric for simple shapes, so stitch ¼in (6mm) seams using the machine needle plate, a ¼in (6mm) wide machine foot, or tape stuck to the machine as a guide. Pin two patches with right sides together, matching edges.

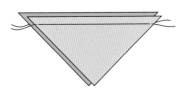

For some shapes, particularly diamonds you need to match the sewing lines, not the fabric edges. Place 2 diamonds right sides together but offset so that the sewing lines intersect at the correct position. Use pins to secure for sewing.

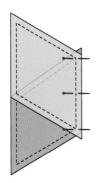

Set your machine at 10–12 stitches per inch (2.5cm) and stitch seams from edge to edge, removing pins as you feed the fabric through the machine.

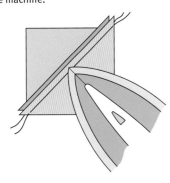

2 Press the seams of each patchwork block to one side before attempting to join it to another block. When joining diamond shaped blocks you will need to offset the blocks in the same way as diamond shaped patches, matching the sewing lines, not the fabric edges.

3 When joining rows of blocks, make sure that adjacent seam allowances are pressed in opposite directions to reduce bulk and make matching easier. Pin pieces together directly through the stitch line and to the right and left of the seam. Remove pins as you sew. Continue pressing seams to one side as you work.

## Hand piecing

1 Pin two patches with right sides together, so that the marked seam lines are facing outwards.

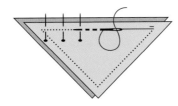

2 Using a single strand of strong thread, secure the corner of a seam line with a couple of back stitches.

3 Sew running stitches along the marked line, working 8–10 stitches per inch (2.5cm) and ending at the opposite seam line corner with a few back stitches. When hand piecing never stitch over the seam allowances.

4 Press the seams to one side, as shown in machine piecing (Step 2).

## MACHINE APPLIQUÉ WITH ADHESIVE WEB

To make appliqué very easy you can use adhesive web (which comes attached to a paper backing sheet) to bond the motifs to the background fabric. There are two types of web available: the first keeps the pieces in place while they are stitched, the second permanently attaches the pieces so that no sewing is required. Follow steps 1 and 2 for the non-sew type and steps 1–3 for the type that requires sewing.

1 Trace the reversed appliqué design onto the paper side of the adhesive web leaving a ¼in (6mm) gap between all the shapes. Roughly cut out the motifs ⅛in (3mm) outside your drawn line.

2 Bond the motifs to the reverse of your chosen fabrics. Cut out on the drawn line with very sharp scissors. Remove the backing paper by scoring the centre of the motif carefully with a scissor point and peeling the paper away from the centre out (to prevent damage to the edges). Place the motifs onto the background, noting any which may be layered. Cover with a clean cloth and bond with a hot iron (check instructions for temperature setting as adhesive web can vary depending on the manufacturer).

3 Using a contrasting or toning coloured thread in your machine, work small close zigzag stitches (or a blanket stitch if your machine has one) around the edge of the

motifs; the majority of the stitching should sit on the appliqué shape. When stitching up to points stop with the machine needle in the down position, lift the foot of your machine, pivot the work, lower the foot and continue to stitch. Make sure all the raw edges are stitched.

## HAND APPLIQUÉ

Good preparation is essential for speedy and accurate hand appliqué. The finger-pressing method is suitable for needle-turning application, used for simple shapes like leaves and flowers. Using a card template is the best method for bold simple motifs such as circles.

### Finger–pressing method

1 To make your template, transfer the appliqué design using carbon paper on to stiff card, and cut out the template. Trace around the outline of your appliquéd shape on to the right side of your fabric using a well sharpened pencil. Cut out shapes, adding by eye a ¼in (6mm) seam allowance all around.

2 Hold shape right side up and fold under the seam, turning along your drawn line, pinch to form a crease. Dampening the fabric makes this very easy. When using shapes with 'points' such as leaves, turn in the seam allowance at the 'point' first, as shown in the diagram. Then continue all round the shape. If your shapes have sharp curves, you can snip the seam allowance to ease the curve. Take care not to stretch the appliqué shapes as you work.

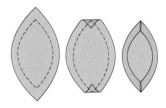

### Card template method

1 Cut out appliqué shapes as shown in step 1 of finger-pressing. Make a circular template from thin cardboard, without seam allowances.

**2** Using a matching thread, work a row of running stitches close to the edge of the fabric circle. Place a thin cardboard template in the centre of the fabric circle on the wrong side of the fabric.

**3** Carefully pull up the running stitches to gather up the edge of the fabric circle around the cardboard template. Press, so that no puckers or tucks appear on the right side. Then, carefully pop out the cardboard template without distorting the fabric shape.

### Straight stems

Place fabric face down and simply press over the ¼in (6mm) seam allowance along each edge. You don't need to finish the ends of stems that are layered under other appliqué shapes. Where the end of the stem is visible, simply tuck under the end and finish neatly.

### Needle-turning application

Take the appliqué shape and pin in position. Stroke the seam allowance under with the tip of the needle as far as the creased pencil line, and hold securely in place with your thumb. Using a matching thread, bring the needle up from the back of the block into the edge of the shape and proceed to blind-hem in place. (This stitch allows the motifs to appear to be held on invisibly.) To do this, bring the thread out from below through the folded edge of the motif, never on the top. The stitches must be small, even and close together to prevent the seam allowance from unfolding and from frayed edges appearing. Try to avoid pulling the stitches too tight, as this will cause the motifs to pucker up. Work around the whole shape, stroking under each small section before sewing.

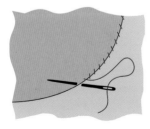

## QUILTING

When you have finished piecing your patchwork and added any borders, press it carefully. It is now ready for quilting.

### Marking quilting designs and motifs

Many tools are available for marking quilting patterns, check the manufacturer's instructions for use and test on scraps of fabric from your project. Use an acrylic ruler for marking straight lines.

### Stencils

Some designs require stencils, these can be made at home, by transferring the designs on to template plastic, or stiff cardboard. The design is then cut away in the form of long dashes, to act as guides for both internal and external lines. These stencils are a quick method for producing an identical set of repeated designs.

### Preparing the backing and batting

• Remove the selvedges and piece together the backing fabric to form a backing at least 4in (10cm) larger all round than the patchwork top.

• Choose a fairly thin batting, preferably pure cotton, to give your quilt a flat appearance. If your batting has been rolled up, unroll it and let it rest before cutting it to the same size as the backing.

• For a large quilt it may be necessary to join two pieces of batting to fit. Lay the pieces of batting on a flat surface so that they overlap by around 8in (20cm). Cut a curved line through both layers.

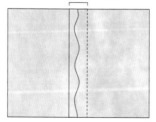

overlap wadding

• Carefully peel away the two narrow pieces and discard. Butt the curved cut edges back together. Stitch the two pieces together using a large herringbone stitch.

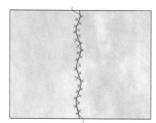

## BASTING THE LAYERS TOGETHER

**1** On the floor or on a large work surface, lay out the backing with wrong side uppermost. Use weights along the edges to keep it taut.

**2** Lay the batting on the backing and smooth it out gently. Next lay the patchwork top, right side up, on top of the batting and smooth gently until there are no wrinkles. Pin at the corners and at the midpoints of each side, close to the edges.

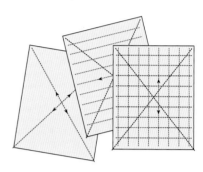

**3** Beginning at the centre, baste diagonal lines outwards to the corners, making your stitches about 3in (7.5cm) long. Then, again starting at the centre, baste horizontal and vertical lines out to the edges. Continue basting until you have basted a grid of lines about 4in (10cm) apart over the entire quilt.

**4** For speed, when machine quilting, some quilters prefer to baste their quilt sandwich layers together using rust-proof safety pins, spaced at 4in (10cm) intervals over the entire quilt.

## HAND QUILTING

This is best done with the quilt mounted on a quilting frame or hoop, but as long as you have basted the quilt well, a frame is not essential. With the quilt top facing upwards, begin at the centre of the quilt and make even running stitches following the design. It is more important to make even stitches on both sides of the quilt than to make small ones. Start and finish your stitching with back stitches and bury the ends of your threads in the batting.

## MACHINE QUILTING

• For a flat looking quilt, always use a walking foot on your machine for stitching straight lines, and a darning foot for free–motion quilting.

• It is best to start your quilting at the centre of the quilt and work out towards the borders, doing the straight quilting lines first (stitch-in-the-ditch) followed by the free-motion quilting.

• When free motion-quilting stitch in a loose meandering style as shown in the diagrams. Do not stitch too closely as this will make the quilt feel stiff when finished. If you wish you can include floral themes or follow shapes on the printed fabrics for added interest.

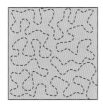

• Make it easier for yourself by handling the quilt properly. Roll up the excess quilt neatly to fit under your sewing machine arm, and use a table or chair to help support the weight of the quilt that hangs down the other side.

## FINISHING

### Preparing to bind the edges

Once you have quilted or tied your quilt sandwich together, remove all the basting stitches. Then, baste around the outer edge of the quilt ¼in (6mm) from the edge of the top patchwork layer. Trim the back and batting to the edge of the patchwork and straighten the edge of the patchwork if necessary.

### Making the binding

**1** Cut bias or straight grain strips the width required for your binding, making sure the grain-line is running the correct way on your straight grain strips. Cut enough strips until you have the required length to go around the edge of your quilt.

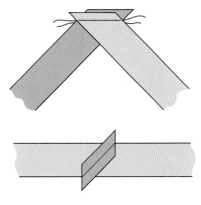

**2** To join strips together, the two ends that are to be joined must be cut at a 45 degree angle, as above. Stitch right sides together, trim turnings and press seam open.

### Binding the edges

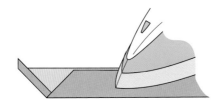

**1** Cut the starting end of binding strip at a 45 degree angle, fold a ¼in (6mm) turning to wrong side along cut edge and press in place. With wrong sides together, fold strip in half lengthways, keeping raw edges level, and press.

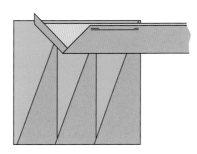

**2** Starting at the centre of one of the long edges, place the doubled binding on to the right side of the quilt keeping raw edges level. Stitch the binding in place starting ¼in (6mm) in from the diagonal folded edge. Reverse stitch to secure, and work ¼in (6mm) in from edge of the quilt towards first corner of quilt. Stop ¼in (6mm) in from corner and work a few reverse stitches.

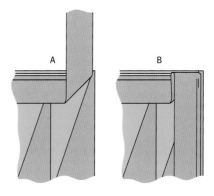

**3** Fold the loose end of the binding up, making a 45 degree angle (see A). Keeping the diagonal fold in place, fold the binding back down, aligning the raw edges with the next side of the quilt. Starting at the point where the last stitch ended, stitch down the next side (see B).

**4** Continue to stitch the binding in place around all the quilt edges in this way, tucking the finishing end of the binding inside the diagonal starting section.

**5** Turn the folded edge of the binding on to the back of the quilt. Hand stitch the folded edge in place just covering binding machine stitches, and folding a mitre at each corner

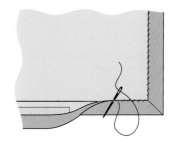

# glossary of terms

**Adhesive or fusible web** This comes attached to a paper backing sheet and is used to bond appliqué motifs to a background fabric. There are 2 types of web available, the first keeps the pieces in place whilst they are stitched, the second permanently attaches the pieces so that no sewing is required.

**Appliqué** The technique of stitching fabric shapes on to a background to create a design. It can be applied either by hand or machine with a decorative embroidery stitch, such as buttonhole, or satin stitch.

**Backing** The bottom layer of a quilt sandwich. It is made of fabric pieced to the size of the quilt top with the addition of about 4in (10.25cm) all around to allow for quilting take-up.

**Basting or tacking** This is a means of holding two fabric layers or the layers of a quilt sandwich together temporarily with large hand stitches, or pins.

**Batting or wadding** This is the middle layer, or padding in a quilt. It can be made of cotton, wool, silk or synthetic fibres.

**Bias** The diagonal grain of a fabric. This is the direction which has the most give or stretch, making it ideal for bindings, especially on curved edges.

**Binding** A narrow strip of fabric used to finish off the edges of quilts or projects; it can be cut on the straight grain of a fabric or on the bias.

**Block** A single design unit that when stitched together with other blocks create the quilt top. It is most often a square, hexagon, or rectangle, but it can be any shape. It can be pieced or plain.

**Border** A frame of fabric stitched to the outer edges of the quilt top. Borders can be narrow or wide, pieced or plain. As well as making the quilt larger, they unify the overall design and draw attention to the central area.

**Chalk pencils** Available in various colours, they are used for marking lines, or spots on fabric.

**Cutting mat** Designed for use with a rotary cutter, it is made from a special 'self-healing' material that keeps your cutting blade sharp. Cutting mats come in various sizes and are usually marked with a grid to help you line up the edges of fabric and cut out larger pieces.

**Design wall** Used for laying out fabric patches before sewing. A large wall or folding board covered with flannel fabric or cotton batting in a neutral shade (dull beige or grey work well) will hold fabric in place so that an overall view can be taken of the placement.

**Free-motion quilting** Curved wavy quilting lines stitched in a random manner. Stitching diagrams are often given for you to follow as a loose guide.

**Fussy cutting** This is when a template is placed on a particular motif, or stripe, to obtain interesting effects. This method is not as efficient as strip cutting, but yields very interesting results.

**Grain** The direction in which the threads run in a woven fabric. In a vertical direction it is called the lengthwise grain, which has very little stretch. The horizontal direction, or crosswise grain is slightly stretchy, but diagonally the fabric has a lot of stretch. This grain is called the bias. Wherever possible the grain of a fabric should run in the same direction on a quilt block and borders.

**Grain lines** These are arrows printed on templates which should be aligned with the fabric grain.

**Inset seams or setting-in** A patchwork technique whereby one patch (or block) is stitched into a 'V' shape formed by the joining of two other patches (or blocks).

**Patch** A small shaped piece of fabric used in the making of a patchwork pattern.

**Patchwork** The technique of stitching small pieces of fabric (patches) together to create a larger piece of fabric, usually forming a design.

**Pieced quilt** A quilt composed of patches.

**Quilting** Traditionally done by hand with running stitches, but for speed modern quilts are often stitched by machine. The stitches are sewn through the top, wadding and backing to hold the three layers together. Quilting stitches are usually worked in some form of design, but they can be random.

**Quilting hoop** Consists of two wooden circular or oval rings with a screw adjuster on the outer ring. It stabilises the quilt layers, helping to create an even tension.

**Reducing Glass** Used for viewing the complete composition of a quilt at a glance. It works like a magnifier in reverse. A useful tool for checking fabric placement before piecing a quilt.

**Rotary cutter** A sharp circular blade attached to a handle for quick, accurate cutting. It is a device that can be used to cut several of fabric at one time. It must be used in conjunction with a 'self-healing' cutting mat and a thick plastic ruler.

**Rotary ruler** A thick, clear plastic ruler marked with lines in imperial or metric measurements. Sometimes they also have diagonal lines indicating 45 and 60 degree angles. A rotary ruler is used as a guide when cutting out fabric pieces using a rotary cutter.

**Sashing** A piece or pieced sections of fabric interspaced between blocks.

**Sashing posts** When blocks have sashing between them the corner squares are known as sashing posts.

**Selvedges** Also known as selvages, these are the firmly woven edges down each side of a fabric length. Selvedges should be trimmed off before cutting out your fabric, as they are more liable to shrink when the fabric is washed.

**Stitch-in-the-ditch or Ditch quilting** Also known as quilting-in-the-ditch. The quilting stitches are worked along the actual seam lines, to give a pieced quilt texture.

**Template** A pattern piece used as a guide for marking and cutting out fabric patches, or marking a quilting, or appliqué design. Usually made from plastic or strong card that can be reused many times. Templates for cutting fabric usually have marked grain lines which should be aligned with the fabric grain.

**Threads** One hundred percent cotton or cotton-covered polyester is best for hand and machine piecing. Choose a colour that matches your fabric. When sewing different colours and patterns together, choose a medium to light neutral colour, such as grey or ecru. Specialist quilting threads are available for hand and machine quilting.

**Walking foot or Quilting foot** This is a sewing machine foot with dual feed control. It is very helpful when quilting, as the fabric layers are fed evenly from the top and below, reducing the risk of slippage and puckering.

**Yo-Yos** A circle of fabric double the size of the finished puff is gathered up into a rosette shape.

## ACKNOWLEDGEMENTS

We are immensely grateful to Lord and Lady St Germans (featured in the portrait, right) for generously allowing us to photograph the quilts in this book at Port Eliot in Cornwall. Their exquisite house, park and gardens are Grade 1 listed, with parts dating back 1500 years, and they are open to the public in the spring and summer each year. They will be holding their hugely popular literary and musical festival in July 2014. For more information on opening dates and times, or to book group tours, contact the Port Eliot Estate Office, St Germans, Saltash,Cornwall, PL12 5ND. Telephone: +0044 (0) 1503 230211. E-mail: info@porteliot.co.uk.

The fabric collection can be viewed online at

**www.coatscrafts.co.uk** *and* **www.westminsterfabrics.com**

**OTHER ROWAN TITLES AVAILABLE**
Kaffe Fassett's *Quilt Romance*
Kaffe Fassett's *Quilts en Provence*
Kaffe Fassett's *Quilts in Sweden*
*Kaffe Quilts Again*

Rowan 100% cotton premium thread, Anchor embroidery thread, and Prym sewing aids, distributed by
Coats Crafts UK, Green Lane Mill, Holmfirth, West Yorkshire, HD9 2DX.
Tel: +44 (0) 1484 681881 • Fax: +44 (0) 1484 687920

Rowan 100% cotton premium thread and Anchor embroidery thread distributed in the USA by
Westminster Fibers, 3430 Toringdon Way, Charlotte, North Carolina 28277.
Tel: 704 329 5800 • Fax: 704 329 5027

Prym productions distributed in the USA by
Prym-Dritz Corp, 950 Brisack Road, Spartanburg, SC 29303.
Tel: +1 864 576 5050 • Fax: +1 864 587 3353
email: pdmar@teleplex.net

Rowan/Coats Crafts UK, Green Lane Mill, Holmfirth,
West Yorkshire HD9 2DX, England.
Tel: +44 (0) 1484 681881 • Email: ccuk.sales@coats.com
www.coatscrafts.co.uk • www.knitrowan.co.uk

Westminster Lifestyle Fabrics, 3430 Toringdon Way, Suite 301,
Charlotte, NC, U.S.A
Tel: 704-329-5800 • Email: fabric@westminsterfibers.com
www.westminsterfabrics.com

# distributors and stockists

Overseas distributors of Rowan fabrics

**AUSTRIA**
Coats Harlander Ges.m.b.H
Autokaderstraße 29, BT2, 1.OG
1210 Wien
Tel.: 00800 26272800
Email: coats.harlander@coats.com
www.coatscrafts.at

**AUSTRALIA**
XLN Fabrics
2/21 Binney Road,
Kings Park
New South Wales 2148
Tel: 61-2 -9621-3066
Email: info@xln.co.zu

**BENELUX**
c/o Coats GmbH
Kaiserstr. 1
79341 Kenzingen
Germany
Tel: +32 (0) 800 77892 (Belgium)
Tel: +31 (0) 800 0226648 (Netherlands)
Tel: +49 (0) 7644 802222 (Luxembourg)
Email: sales.coatsninove@coats.com
www.coatscrafts.be

**BRAZIL**
Coats Corrente Ltda
Rua Do Manifesto,
705 Ipiranga
Sao Paulo
SP 04209-00
Tel: 5511-3247-8000
www.coatscrafts.br

**BULGARIA, GREECE, CYPRUS**
Coats Bulgaria EOOD
7 Magnaurska shkola Str.
1784 Sofia, Bulgaria
Tel: +359 2 976 77 72
Email: officebg@coats.com
www.coatsbulgaria.bg (Bulgaria)
www.coatscrafts.gr (Greece)
www.coatscrafts.com.cy (Cyprus)

**CZECH REPUBLIC**
Coats Czecho s.r.o.
Staré Mesto 246
56932 Staré Mesto
Czech Republic
Tel: 00420 461 616633
Email: galanterie@coats.com
www.coatscrafts.cz

**DENMARK**
Industrial Textiles A/S
Engholm Parkvej 1
DK-3450 Allerod
Denmark
Tel: +45 48 17 20 55
Email: mail@indutex.dk

**ESTONIA**
Coats Eesti As
Ampri tee 9/4 P.K. 2100 Haabneeme
74011 Vlimsi Vald, Harjumaa
Tel: +372 6306 252
www.coatscrafts.co.ee

**FINLAND**
Coats Opti Crafts Oy
Ketjutie 3
04220 Kerava
Tel: 358-9-274871
www.coatscrafts.fi

**FRANCE**
Coats France
Division Arts du Fil
c/o Coats GmbH
Kaiserstr. 1
79341 Kenzingen
Germany
Tel: 0810 060002
Email: artsdufil@coats.com
www.coatscrafts.fr

**3B COM**
7 Rue André Clou
Centre de Gros – Avenue Larrieu
31094 Toulouse Cedex 1
Tel: 33 5 62202096
Email : commercial–3bcom@wanadoo.fr

**GERMANY**
Coats GmbH
Kaiserstraße 1
79341 Kenzingen
Tel: +49 (0) 7644 802222
Email: kenzingen.vertrieb@coats.com
www.coatsgmbh.de

**HUNGARY**
Coats Crafts Hungary Kft.
H-7500 Nagyatad
Gyar utca 21
Tel: (36) 12332197
www.coatscrafts.hu

**ITALY**
Coats Cucirini Srl
Viale Sarca 223
20126 Milano Mi
Tel: +3902 63615210
www.coatscucirini.com

**JAPAN**
Kiyohara & Co Ltd
4-5-2 Minamikyuhoji-Machi
Chuo-Ku
Osaka
541-8506
Tel: 81 6 6251 7179

**LATVIA**
Coats Latvija SIA
Mükusalas iela 41 b
Rïga LV-1004
Tel: +371 67625031
Email: info@coats.lv
www.coatscrafts.lv

**LITHUANIA**
Coats Lietuva UAB
A.Juozapaviciaus g. 6/2,
LT-09310 Vilinius
Tel: 3705- 2730972
www.coatscrafts.lt

**NEW ZEALAND**
Fabco Limited
280 School Road
P.O. Box 84-002
Westgate
Auckland 1250
Tel: 64-9-411-9996
Email: info@fabco.co.nz

**NORWAY**
Industrial Textiles A/S
Engholm Parkvej 1
DK-3450 Allerod
Denmark
Tel: +45 48 17 20 55
Email: mail@indutex.dk

**POLAND**
Coats Polska Sp.z.o.o
ul. Kaczencowa 16
91-214 Lodz
Tel: 48 42 254 0400
www.coatscrafts.pl

**PORTUGAL**
Companhia de Linha Coats & Clark, SA
Quinta de Cravel
4430-968 Vila Nova de Gaia
Tel: 00 351-223 770 700

**SINGAPORE**
Quilts and Calicos
163 Tanglin Road
03-13 Tanglin Mall
247933
Tel: 00 65-688 74708

**SLOVAK REPUBLIC**
Coats s.r.o.
Kopcianska 94
85101 Bratislava
Tel: 00421 2 6820 1061
Email: galanteria@coats.com
www.coatscrafts.sk

**SOUTH AFRICA**
Arthur Bales PTY Ltd
62 4th Avenue
PO Box 44644
Linden 2104
Tel: 27-11-888-2401

**SPAIN**
Coats Fabra, S.A.
Sant Adria, 20
E-08030 Barcelona
Tel: 00 +34 93-290 84 00
www.coatscrafts.es

**SWITZERLAND**
Coats Stroppel AG
Stroppelstrasse 20
5417 Untersiggenthal
Tel: 00800 26272800
Email: coats.stroppel@coats.com
www.coatscrafts.ch

**SWEDEN**
Industrial Textiles A/S
Engholm Parkvej 1
DK-3450 Allerod
Denmark
Tel: +45 48 17 20 55
Email: mail@indutex.dk

**TAIWAN**
Long Teh Trading Co
No. 71 Hebei W. St.
Taichung City
Tel: 886-4-225-6698

**TURKEY**
Coats
Kavacik Mah
Ekinciler Cad
Mecip Fazil SK. No. 8
Istanbul
Tel: +90 216 425 8810
www.coatsturkiye.com.tr

**UK**
Rowan/Coats Crafts UK
Green Lane Mill
Holmfirth
West Yorkshire
HD9 2DX
Tel: 01484 681881
Email: ccuk.sales@coats.com
www.coatscrafts.co.uk

**U.S.A/Canada**
Westminster Lifestyle Fabrics
3430 Toringdon Way
Suite 301
Charlotte
NC
Tel: 704-329-5800
Email: fabric@westminsterfibers.com
www.westminsterfabrics.com